DIABOLIC WARS

BY

HIS HOLINESS POPE SHENOUDA III

St Shenouda Monastery

Sydney, Australia

Diabolic Wars

By His Holiness Pope Shenouda III

Second Edition, September 2019

First Edition August 1989 Translated by Wedad Abbas and revised by Dr. Angeile Botros Samaan

Revised by COEPA 1997

Fully revised and edited by:

St. Shenouda Monastery

8419 Putty Rd, Putty, NSW, 2330

Australia

ISBN: 978-0-6481234-4-6

Special thanks to all the youth who helped, God reward you all.

All scripture quotations, unless otherwise indicated, are taken from the New King James Version. Copyright © 1982 by Thomas Nelson, Inc. Used by permission. All rights reserved.

H.H. Pope Shenouda III
117th Pope of Alexandria and the See of St. Mark

CONTENTS

HISTORY OF THIS BOOK	8
CHAPTER 1	9
THE NATURE OF DIABOLIC WAR	
CHAPTER 2	21
THE DEVIL'S ATTRIBUTES IN HIS WARS	
CHAPTER 3	49
THE INTRIGUES OF THE DEVIL	
CHAPTER 4	142
HOW TO OVERCOME DIABOLIC WARS	
CHAPTER 5	178
BENEFITS OF DIABOLIC WARS	

HISTORY OF THIS BOOK

Many are the sermons I delivered on 'Spiritual Wars'. This part about 'Diabolic Wars' is based on nine sermons delivered on the following dates:

- Two sermons on 'Diabolic Wars' given on Friday 27 March 1970 and Friday 10 April 1970.
- Three sermons which are contemplations on the words, *"Deliver us from the intrigues of the adversary"*. These sermons are part of my contemplations on the Eleventh Hour prayer of the Agpeya, given on Friday 4 August 1972, Friday 11 August 1972 and Friday 18 August 1972.
- A sermon on the war of the devil, given in Lent on Friday evening, 2 March 1973, entitled, *"We begin and he begins with us"*.
- A sermon entitled, *"Away with you, Satan"*, delivered in Lent of the year 1974.
- A sermon on 'Spiritual Wars', given on the evening of Friday 7 March 1980.
- Selections from some sermons on, "The life of purity", "War of classifications" and "The devil modifies his plans".

CHAPTER1

THE NATURE OF DIABOLIC WAR

Spiritual wars are allowed by God for our benefit, for we gain crowns in heaven for succeeding in our struggle here on earth. As one of the saints said;

"None shall be crowned except the one who conquers and none shall conquer except the one who fights."

God intends these wars to test what we will freely choose through our own will and to give us the opportunity to prove ourselves worthy of the riches of the Kingdom of Heaven. As for the devil, it is his nature to resist God's Kingdom and fight against those who seek it. He attempts to war against God through us, God's children, accusing us of being treated too easily, as in the case of Job the just (Job 1, 2). He envies those who lead a life of righteousness and hopes that they do not gain the divine blessing which he deprived himself of.

Diabolic wars are fought against all; no one escapes from them.

When we speak of diabolic wars, we mean those wars waged by the devil, his forces and supporters.

Since the days of Adam, Eve and their son Cain, the devil has been fighting against man, trying his best to condemn man to eternal death and he has, in some cases, succeeded; overthrowing prophets, Apostles and some great characters of the Old Testament - fighting those who had the Spirit of the Lord, such as David and Samson (who both repented) and King Saul, whom God refused and from whom the Spirit of the Lord departed; *"...and a distressing spirit from the LORD troubled him,"* (1 Sam. 16:14).

So, do not think that diabolic wars are directed only at beginners or sinners.

Satan fights against all, especially those who are seeking to grow and are growing in virtue. Thus, all must be on their guard and not think themselves to be above certain wars. Remember that David the prophet was fought and overcome by adultery despite:
- having the Spirit of the Lord
- having been the anointed of the Lord and
- being a man after the Lord's own heart (1 Sam. 13:14, Acts 13:22). The devil will seek any prey.

St. Peter described the devil with these grave words; *"...your adversary the devil walks about like a roaring lion, seeking whom he may devour,"* (1 Pet. 5:8). He wanders about continually to seek and overthrow his prey. When the Lord asked Satan (in the story of Job), *"From where do you come?"* he answered plainly, *"From going to and fro on the earth and from walking up and down on it."* (Job 1:7, 2:2).

The devil does not lose hope, no matter the strength of the person he fights.

It is even said of sin (and by affiliation, the devil), *"...she has cast down many wounded, and all who were slain by her were strong men."* (Prov. 7:26). The devil did not even hesitate to fight against the twelve Disciples of Christ. St. Peter, whom we call the foremost among the Apostles, was cautioned by the Lord; *"Satan has asked for you, that he may sift you as wheat, But I have prayed for you, that your faith should not fail."* (Luke 22:31-32). Elijah, the great prophet, whom God lifted to the heavens, was said by St. James to be, *"...a man with a nature like ours..."* (Jam. 5:17*)*.

The devil even dared to tempt the Lord Jesus Christ Himself.

The devil used three temptations (Matt. 4:1-11). He was not deterred by what he knew about Christ or by the divine revelations which preceded this at the time of His baptism (Matt. 3:13-17); he fought Him throughout the forty days (Mark 1:13, Luke 4:2).

Thus, it was said that the Lord Jesus Christ, *"...was in all points tempted as we are, yet without sin."* (Heb. 4:15), and *"For in that He Himself has suffered, being tempted, He is able to aid those who are tempted."* (Heb. 2:18).

Indeed, the temptation of Christ by Satan is a comfort for us in all our trials. If a temptation befalls you, do not be troubled, for as Christ was tempted and conquered his temptations, you also will conquer.

Diabolic wars are aimed against God Himself, against His kingdom and against us who are His blessed temples.

The devil wants to resist God's Kingdom by any means necessary and rejoices when he is able to overthrow *"...if possible, even the elect."* (Matt. 24:24).

Just as, *"...there is joy in the presence of the angels of God over one sinner who repents...."* (Luke 15:10), undoubtedly the devils rejoice when one righteous person falls and delight when someone submits to them.

St. Paul the Apostle explains these spiritual wars; *"Put on the whole armor of God, that you may be able to stand against the wiles of the devil. For we do not wrestle against flesh and blood, but against principalities, against powers, against the rulers of the darkness of this age, against spiritual hosts of wickedness in the heavenly places."* (Eph. 6:11-12).

St. Paul explained that these spiritual wars need spiritual weapons to resist them, which the Apostle mentions in the same chapter in detail. They require God's help, as He says, *"...without Me you can do nothing."* (John 15:5). In these spiritual wars, how nice it would be to remember the words of David the Prophet, *"...the battle is the Lord's,..."* (1 Sam. 17:47).

Spiritual wars are continuous; they may vary but never end.

As long as you are in the flesh, you are subject to these wars which will continue with you until death. Thus, St. Peter the Apostle says, *"...conduct yourselves throughout the time of your stay here in fear,..."* (1 Pet. 1:17). By 'fear' he does not mean the dread of devils but rather the kind of fear which leads to humility; to the recognition of your weakness.

For individuals, the war continues till death but for the world the war continues forever until the end of all ages. Even when the devil is loosed from his prison, he shall go out to deceive the nations (Rev. 20:7-8). *"In the latter times, some shall depart from the faith..."* (1 Tim. 4:1), and, *"...perilous times shall come."* (2 Tim. 3:1).

Before the coming of Christ, there shall first be a falling away (2 Thess. 2:3) and the devil will come down to earth,

"...having great wrath, because he knows that he has a short time." (Rev 12:12) and will seek out who he may destroy and take with him to his kingdom.

This constant war of the devil may become more severe during times of greater spirituality.

The devil gets very annoyed when we start any spiritual work and uses all his means to deter this kind of work, lest his prey should escape him. Thus, when we start any spiritual work, the devil also starts his work, using his weapons of war.

We begin our spiritual work and he begins his resistance.

He does not feel at ease as long as we have any form of relationship with God, knowing that this endangers his kingdom. Here are some wonderful words from "The Paradise of the Fathers" - *"When the bell rings in the middle of night for prayers, **it does not only awake the monks to pray but the devils are also aroused** to fight monks and prevent them from praying..."* And thus in like manner St. Evagrius said;

"When you begin a holy prayer, be ready for whatever may befall you."

Whenever we start spiritual practices, whether prayers, contemplation, hymns, spiritual reading or kneeling down in worship, the devil does not stand idle. True indeed are the words of the Book of Sirach, quoting Joshua, who was the son of Sirach;

"My son, if you draw near to serve the Lord, prepare your soul for temptation." (Sir. 2:1). This verse is a part of a reading recited on the ordination of a new monk. It is also included in the reading of the Third Hour of Tuesday of Passion Week. Of course, the devil gets ready to fight those who are ready to resist him. Thus, do not be astonished at the wars which accompany spiritual work. Never let such wars cause you to turn back but be vigorous and steadfast in order to withstand any trouble that comes upon you, remembering the words of St. Paul the Apostle, *"...be steadfast, immovable, always abounding in the work of the Lord, knowing that your labor is not in vain in the Lord."* (1 Cor. 15:58).

We start the struggle and he starts fighting. We begin our spiritual work and he begins his resistance.

An example of this is that the devil gets annoyed at fasting because through it, *"... I discipline my body and bring it into subjection..."* (1 Cor. 9:27) so that the soul may rise and attain God - the devil hates this. He gets annoyed during Lent because people are very devout during this time. Lent also reminds the devil of the fasting of the Lord Jesus Christ and of his own defeat (Matt. 4). Thus, the devil struggles to hinder this fasting or raises problems during it so that people may be engaged in those problems and neglect spiritual work.

Hence, some people find that during Lent there are more problems and trials.

Undoubtedly, spiritual work stirs up the envy of the devil.

The devil envies a spiritual person for his attachment to God, an attachment which he is deprived of. He envies man because although he is earthly and has flesh, he attempts to elevate his spirit so that the flesh can be made subject to it. While the devil, despite being a spirit (Matt. 12:45) is far away from God and lives as a evil and unclean spirit (Mark 1:27).

From the beginning the devil envied Adam and Eve, making them fall into sin and the condemnation of death. Thus, we say in the Divine Liturgy, *"...death which entered into the world through the envy of Satan"*.

The devil envies only those who are successful in their spiritual work.

He envies those who are near to God and favoured by Him. He envies the penitents for the zeal of their repentance and the worshippers in their deep attachment to the church. He envies the humble, the meek and the pure-hearted and fights all of them. But what about those who are under his domination and are overcome by sin, or who are lazy in their spiritual life? Why would he fight them? He is satisfied with their condition or puts them under his watch or leads them into what is worse.

Here we mention three main states of spiritual war faced by man:

1) A person is fought directly by the devil.
2) A person fought by his own desires; the devil might have been the starting point but he leaves his prey to be fought by his inner corruption, or by the habits dominating him. Someone might be fought by the body or by his instincts, another by his own self or his own thoughts.
3) The person fought by false brethren, by wicked people or evil surroundings, which we call *'supporters of the devil'* or *'the devil's powers'*.

Thus, the church teaches us to say at the end of the

Thanksgiving prayer, *"All envy, all temptation, all works of Satan, all intrigues of the wicked, and the rising up of enemies, visible and invisible, cast them away from us, and from all your people..."*.

There is another kind of these wars which we may call tests or trials.

An example of this kind is given in the Holy Bible; *"Now it came to pass after these things that God tested Abraham, and said to him... Take now your son, your only son Isaac, whom you love... and offer him there as a burnt offering..."* (Gen 22:2). Here, God was not fighting our father Abraham, God forbid but He was testing his heart to know the depth of his love and his obedience to Him - and our father Abraham succeeded in this test.

The saint and the sinner are both liable to be fought but what is the difference between them?

The main difference is that a saint is exposed to external war only, while his inner self is pure. He does not accept this external war but rather refuses it and resists it with all his power in order to overcome it.

On the other hand, a sinner or a wicked person may be exposed to a war on two fronts - both external and internal. He is exposed to the devil's temptations from the outside and is fought internally by the lusts of his own heart and mind, thus he yields to the devil, opening his interior gates for him, welcoming and accepting his thoughts and suggestions. Even if he still has the conscience to resist, it will be a weak resistance which will not continue long nor will it seriously repel the thoughts of the outer enemy.

When saints are fought, their power is revealed and they conquer, but sinners will find themselves defeated. **However, God may sometimes allow saints to be defeated, temporarily, for their own benefit.**

A person who always conquers may be fought by pride and may think highly of himself! Thus, God sometimes permits that saints be conquered so that they may be humbled. This defeat makes them realise the enemy's power and severity in his wars so that they may learn to have compassion towards their brothers who are exposed to such wars. As St. Paul the apostle says;

"Remember the prisoners as if chained with them; those who are mistreated; since you yourselves are in the body also." (Heb. 13:3).

A person who does not experience diabolic wars may condemn or despise those who fall but one who suffers and toils is kind and compassionate to those who fall, and prays for their salvation as the Apostle says, *"...knowing that the same sufferings are experienced by your brotherhood in the world."* (1 Pet. 5:9).

Indeed, how frightful are the words of Revelation about 'the beast';

"It was granted to him to make war with the saints and to overcome them..." (Rev. 13:7).

And how frightful is what follows "...*And authority was given him over every tribe, tongue, and nation… All who dwell on the earth will worship him, whose names have not been written in the Book of Life of the Lamb slain from the foundation of the world."* (Rev. 13:7-8).

However, lest some should despair, it is stated that those who shall worship him are those whose names are not written in the Book of Life since the establishment of the world.

That is, the sons of perdition, though they are undoubtedly abundant, a matter which demonstrates the severity of the wars of the devil and his powers. We are comforted in this matter by the statement that the beast and the devil were cast into the lake of fire and brimstone (Rev. 20:10).

Yet, we mention all this so that we may be cautious.

Since our enemy is so fierce, let us then hearken to the words of the Apostle, *"See then that you walk circumspectly, not as fools but as wise, redeeming the time, because the days are evil."* (Eph. 5:15-16).

The victories of the devil do not frighten us but make us circumspect and cautious. They force us not to depend on ourselves, as we realise how quickly we fail but:

In our wars, we must cleave to the Lord for help and triumph.

He fights the devil in us and conquers the world in us. Does He not say, *"…be of good cheer, I have overcome the world."* (John 16:33). Yes, He conquered the world when He was tempted by the devil and He still conquers and will conquer the world in all ages for as long as the devil is fighting us. So,

"Now thanks be to God who always leads us in triumph in Christ..." (2 Cor. 2:14).

He conquered the devil in our human nature, sanctifying and blessing it; giving it the spirit of victory. So, we address Him in the Liturgy of St. Gregory saying, *"You have blessed my nature in You"*. The devil had previously conquered this human nature but the Lord Jesus Christ has restored it to its Divine image, demonstrating power and dignity in front of the devils whom he conquered while in our nature.

Thus, the devil no longer considers our nature his 'game', which he can overcome whenever he wants. For since he has been defeated by it, he developed a fear of it.

The Lord has saved us from the spirit of failure and given us power to support us against the wars of the devil. We now have hope that Christ will conquer the devil in us, as when St. Paul says, *"...Christ may dwell in your hearts through faith..."* (Eph. 3:17).

Thus, we do not get troubled by diabolic wars as long as the hand of the Lord is with us, fighting and conquering on our behalf.

God does not repel diabolic wars for us but gives us victory over them.

He fights on our behalf, conquers the devils and then gives us crowns because we submit our wills to Him, while He is fighting the devils for us.

The above is only a simple introduction from which we will proceed to speak about the devil and his craftiness.

CHAPTER 2

THE DEVIL'S ATTRIBUTES IN HIS WARS

We **ought to know the attributes of our enemy and the manner in which he fights in order to know how to fight him.**

What then are the attributes of the devil? How does he fight? Does he have a constant manner of fighting, or does he change his methods according to the circumstances? This is the subject which we want to examine so that we may learn to resist him, *"...lest Satan should take advantage of us; for we are not ignorant of his devices."* (2 Cor. 2:11).

According to the Holy Bible, we know the following about the devil:

1. He is an unceasing fighter.

Since his fall, the devil's main concern has been to wage war. He has always been a fighter. Before overthrowing our forefathers Adam and Eve he overthrew multitudes of heavenly angels who followed him and became his agents.

Since then to overthrow others has become his job.

He began to fight all. He overthrew the angelic Cherubim, principalities, dominions and powers which joined his ranks; he fought God's prophets, apostles and anointed. He also fights the secluded hermits, anchorites, monks and anyone who loves God. He fights whomever he knows to be living a life of righteousness.

He is called the 'opponent' and 'resister' for he resists God's Kingdom and opposes His will. He is also given these titles:

the dragon, the old serpent, Satan and the devil (Rev.12:9); and before the crucifixion he was given the title of *"...the ruler of this world..."* (John 14:30).

He never stops fighting- he neither tires nor rests.

He *"...walks about like a roaring lion,..."* (1 Pet. 5:8). In the story of Job, he told God twice that he had returned, *"From going to and fro on the earth, and from walking back and forth on it."* (Job 1:7, 2:2). He watches his victims continuously and plants his seeds everywhere. Wherever the Lord plants wheat, he comes and plants tares: *"...but while men slept, his enemy came and sowed tares among the wheat and went his way."* (Matt. 13:25).

Not only does he fight men but he fights even the angels.

He contended with Archangel Michael, disputing over the body of Moses the prophet (Jude 9). He resisted one of the angels of the Lord who tried to save Joshua the high priest from him (Zech. 3:1-2). He also resisted the angel whom the Lord sent to Daniel the prophet for 21 days until the Archangel Michael interfered to help him (Dan. 10:12-13). In the Book of Revelations we find a passage which strikes awe in the reader;

"And war broke out in heaven: Michael and his angels fought with the dragon ... and his angels..." **(Rev. 12:7).**

He fights on earth and in the heavens and although all his wars end in his destruction and defeat, he cannot stop fighting because this has become a part of his nature.

Another attribute of the devil is

that:

2. He is powerful.

That is because he is one of the angels, *"Who excel in strength,"* according to the description of the psalmist in Psalm 103:20.

As an angel, he lost his purity but did not lose his powerful nature.

Thus, the Apostle described him as *"...a roaring lion..."* (1 Pet. 5:8); and in the story of Job, he *"...struck Job with painful boils from the sole of his foot to the crown of his head."* (Job 2:7). He also raised a violent wind which smote the corners of Job's house and it fell upon and killed the young men (Job 1:19). Many spiritual matters prove his power, among these are the following:

a) He was able to mislead the whole world in the days of the flood.

Only one family was saved, that is the family of our father Noah (Gen. 6). God found that the only solution to cleanse the earth from corruption was to destroy every living being from the face of the earth.

b) The same can be said of Sodom.

God did not find even ten righteous persons for whose sake he would have had mercy on that city (Gen. 18:32). He found only the family of Lot – four people – one of whom was Lot's wife who perished outside the city. Lot's two daughters sinned after leaving Sodom, and Lot himself, *"...dwelling among them, tormented his righteous soul from day to day by seeing and hearing their lawless deeds."* (2 Pet. 2:8).

c) The power of the devil is also apparent in that he was able to make most of the world pagan.

He was able to lead all the world, except for the Jewish nation, into paganism in ancient times. Even then the Jewish nation fell, at times, into worshipping idols. When Moses the prophet was on the mountain, his people made for themselves a molded calf and offered burnt offerings to it, saying, *"This is your god, O Israel, that brought you out of the land of Egypt!"* (Ex. 32:1-6).

In the days of Elijah the prophet, during the reign of Ahab the king, there were among God's people four hundred and fifty prophets of Baal and four hundred prophets of the Asherah. This means that there were eight hundred and fifty false prophets who ate at Jezebel's table (1 Kin. 18:19). The Books of Kings and Chronicles tell us that many of the kings of Judah and Israel fell into the worship of idols.

d) The power of the devil is further made apparent in that he was able to make Solomon the wise fall into worshipping idols.

Solomon, the man who was said to be the wisest on the earth (1 Kin. 3:12), to whom God appeared twice (1 Kin. 3:5, 9:2) is said in the Holy Bible to have become a worshipper of idols; *"For it was so, when Solomon was old, that his wives turned* his heart after other gods; and his heart was not loyal to the LORD his God, as was the heart of his father David. For Solomon went after Ashtoreth the goddess of the Sidonians, and after Milcom the abomination of the Ammonites..."* (1 Kin. 11:4-8).

Indeed, how great a tragedy befell Solomon – do not underestimate the extent of the devil's power.

e) Among the proofs of the devil's power is what he will do in the last days.

"...Satan will be released from his prison, and will go out to deceive the nations which are in the four corners of the earth..." (Rev. 20:7-8). He shall even deceive the elect, if possible, through the false christ's and prophets whom he will send with great signs and wonders (Matt. 24:24).

The potency of the devil's work during this time is expressed by the Lord in the following way; *"...unless those days were shortened, no flesh would be saved; but for the elect's sake those days will be shortened."* (Matt. 24:22).

In those days, the devil will also send the anti-christ, the man of sin, who opposes and exalts himself above all that is called God; *"The coming of the lawless one is according to the working of Satan, with all power, signs, and lying wonders, and with all unrighteous deception among those who perish."* (2 Thess. 2: 9-10).

As a result of the devil's power, there will first be a falling away.
This will take place before the coming of Christ (2 Thess. 2:3).

We thank God that those hard days will be shortened and the anti-christ will be consumed by the spirit of the mouth of the Lord and be destroyed with the brightness of His coming (2 Thess. 2:8).

Among the other examples of the devil's power are the following:

He could speak through a great Apostle like St. Peter. The Lord rebuked him when Peter said it was not right for Him to die, saying, *"Get behind Me, Satan! You are an offense to Me."* (Matt. 16:22-23).

He also sifted the twelve apostles as wheat; the Lord prayed specifically that Peter's faith would not fail, as he was the one who was to betray Him (Luke 22:32).

He overthrew men of valour like David and Samson; he destroyed the prophet Balaam and corrupted Demas, one of St. Paul's disciples. All his victims were and are strong - *"All who were slain by her were strong men..."* (Prov. 7:26). The words of David the prophet are true indeed, *"How the mighty have fallen, And the weapons of war perished!"* (2 Sam. 1:27).

Another example of his power is his ability to possess people.

There were (and still are) people who are demon possessed and need the devil to be cast out from them. The Lord said to His disciples concerning these people, *"Cast out devils..."* (Matt. 10:8). One of these people had *"Legion"* (Mark 5:9) and *"...neither could any man tame him"* (Mark 5:9).

At that time, the disciples of the Lord were unable to cast out some of these devils, so the Lord said to them, *"...This kind can come out by nothing but prayer and fasting."* (Mark 9:29).

Perhaps because of this power of the devil, God bound him a thousand years;

"...and he cast him into the bottomless pit, and shut him up, and set a seal on him, so that he should deceive the nations no more till the thousand years were finished. But after these things he must be released for a little while,..." (Rev 20:2-3).

This description about the power of the devil should not make you fear him! No.

Though the devil is powerful, God is more powerful than him.

Not only did God subdue the devil for us but He let many of the fathers conquer him and the devil even feared them. We will return to this point in a later chapter.

Another important aspect of the devil's character as our opponent is:

3. He is experienced in fighting and knows our nature.

The devil has been fighting man for more than seven thousand years, since the time of Adam - imagine what experience he has gained from his fight with humanity. Undoubtedly, he is the creature most capable of understanding the human soul and how to fight it. He has examined the human soul very well and knows its strengths and weaknesses, as well as the way to fight it.

The devil is the greatest psychologist and psychoanalyst.

Psychology to him is not mere theories but a practical science which he has practiced on a grand level – on all of humanity. Thus, he knows when he should fight, how to fight and when to wait. He knows the gates to the mind and to the heart.

Other qualities which appear in the devil's wars are:

4. He is intelligent and resourceful.

He is called "*...the old serpent,*" (Rev. 20:2, 12:9) and the Holy Bible says, "*Now the serpent was more cunning that any beast of the field,...*" (Gen. 3:1). He is intelligent and wise in doing evil. Thus the Bible requires us to be "*...wise as serpents,*" (Matt. 10:16). The wisdom of the devil is entirely mischief, malice and subtlety.

The devil's intelligence is made clear in that he changes his plans and methods according to the circumstances. Among his dangerous wiles are; lying, deceit and beguilement which he weaves so intelligently that the person fought cannot be aware of it. He is also able to introduce sin disguised as virtue.

How abundant are the wiles of the devil! We shall allocate for them a special and central chapter in this book

Among the other attributes of the devil are the following:

5. He is a liar.

He lied when he said to our forefathers Adam and Eve, *"You will not surely die."* and *"...you will be like God,"* (Gen. 3:4, 5). Lying is a distinctive characteristic of the devil, thus the Lord said of the devil - *"...for he is a liar and the father of it,..."* (John 8:44). This was said so that we might not believe nor be deceived by anything put forward by the devil. The lies of the devil are not only the words which he utters but there is also something far more dangerous:

There are the false prophets and false christs whom he sends.

The Lord warned us against them, saying, *"Then if anyone says to you, 'Look, here is the Christ!' or 'There!' do not believe it. For false christs and false prophets will rise and show great signs and wonders to deceive, if possible, even the elect."* (Matt. 24:23-24). Of course, the signs and wonders which they will give are from the devil. It is said of the anti-christ, *"The coming of the lawless one is according to the working of Satan, with all power, signs, and lying wonders..."* (2 Thess. 2:9).

The devil speaks through the mouths of the false prophets.
In ensuring King Ahab perished, the devil said, *"I will persuade him.... I will go out and be a lying spirit in the mouth of all his prophets."* (1 Kin. 22:21-22). Just as the Holy Spirit speaks through the mouths of the holy prophets, so the devil speaks through the false prophets.

The devil also tells his lies in false dreams and visions.

How abundant are the wars faced by the monks through such false dreams and visions! Some of these are included in "The Paradise of the Fathers". An example of this is the appearance of the devil to a monk, saying, *"I am the angel Gabriel. The Lord sent me to you"*. But the monk replied humbly, *"I am a sinner; I don't deserve to see an angel. Perhaps you were sent to another monk and lost your way."* The lie was revealed and the devil departed from him.

Another example is his appearance to a monk, saying to him, *"I am Christ. Worship me."* The monk said in his heart, *"I worship my Lord Christ every day. Why then does he ask me to do so now?"* In this way, the deception was discovered; the monk rebuked him and he departed.

How abundant also are the false dreams by which the devil misleads people, making them think that the dreams are from God! St. Paul the Apostle said of these false visions; *"For Satan himself transforms himself into an angel of light."* (2 Cor. 11:14).

In the story of father Galion the anchorite, the devils appeared to him in the form of roaming fathers wishing him to join them. He did not discover that they were devils except when they led him astray in the wilderness, mocking him and leaving him scorned. However due to his devoutness, purity of heart and his previous toil, God had mercy on him and saved him.

The lies of the devil appear also in the words of magicians, diviners, etc.

Thus, the Lord commanded, *"...you shall not learn to follow the abominations of those nations. There shall not be found among you anyone who makes his son or his daughter pass through the fire, or one who practices witchcraft, or a soothsayer, or one who interprets omens, or a sorcerer, or one who conjures spells, or a medium, or a spiritist, or one who calls up the dead. For all who do these things are an abomination to the LORD, and because of these abominations the LORD your God drives them out from before you."* (Deut. 18:9-12).

These verses reveal to us another thing:

The deception of the devil when people consult spirits of the dead and summoning spirits.

In such meetings, he may pretend to be the spirit of a certain person, giving those present some deceiving information which he knows about that person and his family. If they believe him, he begins to tell them gradually things to mislead them, all of which is conjured by the devil to deceive people.

Among his lies also are what he says through the mouths of astrologers and those who claim the knowledge of the unknown.

Whether through astrology, palmistry, geomancy, reading coffee-cups, or fortune-telling by various ways and methods. It is theologically evident that no one but God alone knows the unknown. So whoever claims knowledge of the unknown is untrue.

All the temptations of the devil are kinds of falsehood.

He makes man imagine some happiness to be gained from sin,

whether it be pleasure, authority, benefit, dignity or glory and when one falls, they discover that all the temptations of the devil are merely a mirage and lies. This is what he did with Adam and Eve, making them imagine that they would be like God; and making Solomon imagine that he would be happy with the abundant joys and luxury surrounding him but Solomon found that all was vanity and vexation of spirit (Eccl. 2).

It is always the method of the devil that he adorns the way of sin and gives it beautiful qualities to tempt people into falling into his trap. Yet, all his ornaments are falsehoods through which he hides the ugliness of sin and its evil results.

The daydreams which he offers to his victims are all falsehoods as well.

He offers them these dreams as a kind of pleasure which would drug them against positive work. Thus, they live through these dreams in false imagination, building palaces of sand, imagining glories, pleasures and joys. Then they awake and find nothing of this kind - the devil has wasted their time, detained them from useful work and given them false comfort.

Among the lying schemes of the devil are deluding the person who commits suicide into thinking that death will relieve him from his troubles.

He concentrates on the point that there is no use in this life, that there is no solution for the person's problems but death. He presents death as the only solution by which he can get rid of all his troubles and have comfort. When the person believes him and kills himself, he finds no rest but finds himself in hell, in weariness and pain, unavoidable and incomparable with any worldly troubles. He discovers then that death does not put an end to his troubled life but is the beginning of a more troublesome one. The devil has deceived him through lies, misled him and destroyed him.

Almost all sins are hidden behind one of the devil's lies.

The devil suggests to the thief that no one will see him or discover his theft. He suggests the same thing to the smuggler, the briber and the one who commits fraud. In all this the devil is a liar, for God sees all and everything is revealed before Him.

He suggests to the murderer that the victim deserved to be killed and that his life was a mistake which needed to be corrected, or that murder washes out shame which stains his honor, or that it comforts the soul of a deceased relative.

Perhaps atheism is the greatest falsehood offered by the devil to humanity.

He lied when he suggested to the existentialists that God's existence hinders their own existence. He also suggested to the Marxists that God lives in a high tower and does not care for human society, letting the oppressor oppress and the rich enslave the poor!

Another attribute of the devil is:

6. He is insistent.

The devil does not weary. He may offer a certain thought many, many times and continues to offer it even though it is refused by people.

A person may be made to yield and submit due to the continuous pressure and insistence.

It is stated in "The Paradise of the Fathers" that the devil fought one of the monks with one sin for 50 years without ceasing, getting desperate or getting weary.

Even when he was fighting the Lord Jesus Christ, he did not cease after his failure in the first, second and third temptation. Though the Lord rebuked him and he departed, this departure was temporary – as St. Luke the Evangelist said, *"Now when the devil had ended every temptation, he departed from Him until an opportune time."* (Luke 4:13).

The devil never gets desperate when he fails and is never ashamed but always returns!
When he failed in the first temptation of Job, he demanded again to be allowed to subject him to more difficult temptations; and when he failed in all his temptations of the Lord Jesus Christ, he came to Him when He was on the cross and said, *"If You are the Son of God, come down from the cross,..."* (Matt. 27:40).

The devil is so determined to overthrow people that he does not acknowledge any obstacles.

He did not care that Adam and Eve were created in the image

and likeness of God (Gen. 1).

He did not care that David was the anointed of the Lord, nor that Solomon was the wisest man on earth, nor that Peter the Apostle had a zeal for Christ, nor that Joshua was the high priest (Zech. 3), nor that Aaron was the chief priest (Ex. 32), nor that Samson was consecrated as a Nazarite of the the Lord. He does not care about the positions or spirituality of people but strikes without considering what the result may be. Since he dared to tempt Christ the Lord of Glory, would he not dare to tempt mortals?

He spreads his poison to people seeking to destroy them and waits patiently for the outcome. Though the individual may not perish by it today, the devil patiently waits to see if the individual will perish the next day, the next year or even in the next twenty years.

The devil is persistent, importunate and stubborn. He is not disheartened by failure, nor does he get desperate due to a person's strong faith. He proceeds in his plan to destroy God's Kingdom and to mislead even the elect. If he cannot defile someone's body, he defiles their thoughts. Whoever refuses his attacks on their spirituality is given at least a thorn in the flesh (2 Cor. 12:7). If he cannot overthrow God's children, he at least accuses them and that is why he is called the accuser.

7. The accuser.

In Revelations, he is said to be, *"...the accuser of our brethren, who accused them before our God day and night..."* (Rev. 12:10).

He accuses saints, claiming that he did not have the opportunity to fight them! Or that the opportunity which he did have was not sufficient!

Formerly, he stood before God to accuse Job, claiming that previously he did not have the opportunity to fight him. He said to God, *"Have You not made a hedge around him... You have blessed the work of his hands... But now, stretch out Your hand and touch all that he has, and he will surely curse You to Your face!"* (Job 1:10-11). God confronted the devil, revealing to him the cruelty and falsehood of his accusation and said to him about Job, *"And still he holds fast to his integrity, although you incited Me against him, to destroy him without cause,..."* (Job 2:3). However, the devil continued to accuse him a second time, asking for permission to smite Job with sore boils (Job 2:7).

It is amazing that the devil performs whatever he wants and still complains! He complains in spite of his numerous gifts.

8. He has numerous talents.

He has numerous extraordinary abilities. He knows and has mastered many things.

God did not take away from him the talents and abilities of an angel.

His knowledge is vast. He knows the verses of the Bible very well and uses them in fighting even theologians. In the temptation on the mount, he twisted the meaning of passages in the Holy Bible in order to achieve his goal (Matt. 4:6). He is the author of all heresies and heterodoxies. He put them in the minds of heretics and offered them incorrect interpretations of verses in the Bible. True are the words of St. Athanasius the Apostolic, *"Our enemy is not the Arians but the devil."*

The devil knows poetry and many poets speak of 'the devil of poetry', which inspired them with ideas. It is not strange then that one of the spiritualists said that he was able to call for the spirit of a famous poet to hear him perform a recitation. It is probable that the devil was the inspiration behind the poem and dictated it to the poet in the same way that he recited it!

The devil also knows music, art, carving, drawing and songs.
He can inspire a person to create amusements in any field of art to entice people, overthrow them or lead them astray from their spiritual course.

The devil can be considered among the most distinguished psychologists, or even at the head of them due to his practical experience.

As his experience helps him in his wars, his wars also add to his experience and his knowledge. The devil is not a psychologist of the mind alone but also a spiritualist – a psychologist of things concerning the spirit, for he himself is a spirit.

The knowledge of the devil is used to serve his own purpose.

The purpose of the devil is known - it is to resist God and His Kingdom. He uses all his knowledge to realise this diabolic aim.

Another attribute of the devil is:

9. He is cruel.

He works with incredible cruelty and without a shred of mercy.

His cruelty is very evident in the story of Job the Just.

He also led many to perdition and loss; such as those who were destroyed by the flood, or by the fires of Sodom, or those who were swallowed up alive by the earth (Num. 16).

His cruelty is also evident in that he drives his 'followers' to insanity:

The mad man of the country of Gadarenes *"...had demons for a long time. And he wore no clothes, nor did he live in a house but in the tombs... and he was kept under guard, bound with chains and shackles; and he broke the bonds and was driven by the demon into the wilderness."* (Luke 8:26-29); *"...he was in the mountains and in the tombs, crying out and cutting himself with stones."* (Mark 5:5). There are many others resembling him.

His cruelty appears also in fighting saints and in his frightful appearances.

When fighting St. Anthony the Great, he would appear in very terrible forms, sometimes in the form of wild and horrifying beasts that would make loud and fearful voices. Once, he attacked the saint, leaving him half-dead. Whoever reads the story of St. Kyriakos the roaming anchorite will find other examples which resemble or surpass this kind of war.

He is cruel in the wars, calamities and crimes which he instigates in the world.

The results of all these are known, yet the devil is pleased with all the calamities of the world and counts this as a victory for himself. Besides destroying souls and minds, spreading contentions and causing disruption and dispersion, he takes joy in spreading violence and destruction.

Believe me, if we read about the cruelty of the devil in his terrifying wars against saints, we would realise that what we have endured from the devil is only a trifle in comparison.

What is amazing about the devil's cruelty is that he pretends sometimes to be kind but:

10. He is deceitful in appearing kind.

His kind words are a malicious means to overthrow people.

He 'shows sympathy' for you when you fast and calls you to eat, to sustain your own health! He warns you against diseases and sickness! He says to you, *"Beware, lest you should kill your body, which is a talent with which you may glorify God."* Remember the Apostles' saying, *"For no one ever hated his own flesh, but nourishes and cherishes it..."* (Eph. 5:29).

He 'sympathises' with you when you become spiritually active and when you keep awake in prayers, reading and kneeling down in worship (metanoia), convincing you kindly to go to sleep or rest.

He is so 'kind' that he is anxious about your well being, fears that you may fall into 'extremes' and tries to convince you to limit your struggling.

When you are in deep spiritual practices, he says to you, *"There is no need for all this, the fathers teach us that the middle way has saved many..."*. Accordingly, he says, *"Beware of being too strenuous lest the devil should strike you with a right blow which is harder and lest you should fall in vainglory, which is the worst evil of all vices."* He even uses false warnings by saying, *"Undoubtedly, this strenuousness in struggling is the work of the devil and he does not intend any good for you! Hearken to the words of the Holy Bible, "Do not be overly righteous, Nor be overly wise: Why should you destroy yourself?"* (Eccl. 7:16)".

The 'kind-hearted' devil pities you when you weep for your sins...

He says to you, *"Why do you weep and live in sadness? This is not the way of God... Did not God forgive your sins and wash them with His Blood? Why then do you weep for them? Do you want to keep weeping till you destroy your nerves, your soul and be exposed before people? Did not the Holy Bible say, "Rejoice in the Lord always,"* (Phil. 4:4)." He goes on pressing till you lose humility of heart, lose the tears of repentance and become lukewarm spiritually.

Thus, it becomes easy for you to sin and perhaps you return to sinning. Of course, he makes you forget the words of the Bible, *"...by the sadness of the countenance, the heart is made better,"* (Eccl. 7:3).

The 'kind-hearted' devil justifies your mistakes for you so that your conscience may not worry.

He prevents you from rebuking yourself, having regard for your feelings! He is 'compassionate' for you, lest you should fall into sorrow and despair! Thus, in all your mistakes he offers you various excuses and justifications, advising you, *"Do not say of everything, "That is wrong," and do not rebuke yourself exceedingly or this will lead you into paranoia. What you did was wrong but you did not mean it. Your intentions are good and God looks at your intentions. It is wrong but what could you have done? The circumstances were pressing and believe me, if I had been in your place I would have done the same thing. God does not require from you that which is beyond your ability; so do not be distressed."*

By justifying your mistakes he puts your conscience at ease so that you are able to *'swallow a camel'*. He makes you avoid repentance, avoid keeping caution and avoid remaining on guard even in the little things.

The 'kindness' of the devil is not charity but a means of overthrowing people. So beware of him, do not listen to him, be firm and behave cautiously. Be sure that the devil is dishonest in all his wars against you; all advices he offers you are not faithful, although they may appear good. He wants nothing but your perdition.

Another attribute of the devil is:

11. He is envious.

His heart never rests whenever he sees a spiritually successful or righteous person. He tries his best to overthrow such a person.

In his envy, he deals his blows without any mercy...

He envied Joseph the righteous for the visions which he saw and instilled envy in the hearts of Joseph's brothers so that they sold him as a slave. Then he envied him for his success and for the confidence Potiphar placed in him; so he arranged a scheme by which Joseph was placed in prison.

He envied the world for its faith in God and made the world fall into paganism, polytheism and atheism. For this purpose he developed all kinds of philosophies and religions. True are the words of the Psalm, *"For all the gods of the peoples are idols,..."* **(Ps. 96:5).**

The devil envies knowledge, wisdom, chastity, and humility...

He has spread and spreads ignorance, adultery and pride in the world with all the wickedness he possesses. Adultery and pride have become two of greatest traps the devil uses against mankind in order to catch those who escape other sins and those who have yet to fall into these sins. He turned Solomon from his wisdom and made him fall. He threw many wrong ideas into the world until the words of the Psalmist were fulfilled; *"The fool has said in his heart, 'There is no God,...'"* (Ps. 14:1).

The envy of the devil is destructive and not merely a sentiment.

For when the devil envies, he fights with all his might, as in the case of Job. He envied him for his integrity and he accused him before God. He also envied the monks of the wilderness for their hermitage and asceticism and aroused the most severe wars against them. He envied Origen, the most learned of his age and the first professor of Theology at that time. He threw him into many heresies for which the church excommunicated him, and it was said of him, *"Ye, the high tower, how did you fall?". (Is 14:12)*

Hence when you do any act of righteousness, expect the envy of the devils.

Expect that they will never leave you in righteousness but will try to make you fall by all their means. So when they strike you on a day of deep spirituality, do not become despondent but say, *'This is what I expected, However, I pray for God's mercy to help me not to fall again.'*

If God gives you a gift, expect the envy of the devils in this case also.

They will either try to make you fall into pride, or make you use that gift incorrectly, thus losing its spiritual aim and its benefit to you and others.

Another attribute of the devil is:

12. He is an opportunist.

The devil tries to seize every opportunity he can to make you fall into temptation - he took advantage of the hunger of the Lord Jesus Christ after fasting forty days and tempted Him with bread.

He also benefited from the fear of St. Peter and led him to deny Christ.

He took advantage of the Jews who held fast to the Sabbath and made them deny the miracles of Christ, miracles that had never been seen on earth, yet despite this they accused Him of sinning against the law (John 9:11).

13. The devil is unfaithful and dishonest.

As we have said before, the devil may show compassion for your health whether in respect to fasting, vigil/watchfulness or any physical weariness. He advises you to give rest to your body for the sake of your health!

But he is not truly honest in showing concern for your health.

He advises you to take rest and prevents you from keeping vigil but only in respect to prayers, contemplations or spiritual readings. However, if you keep awake in amusement or entertainment, he will not warn you to take rest for your health's' sake but will encourage you!

When you get tired because of vain worldly matters, he

does not advise you to rest.

If you tire of collecting money, of seeking fame and dignity, of running after your lusts and pleasures, of arranging clamorous parties, of games and sports and any other worldly activities his 'compassion' will not be aroused for you, nor would he ask you to rest!

He advises you to rest only when you are tired in a spiritual practice. Your spiritual struggle is the only thing that arouses his 'compassion' for you and your health!

So if he asks you to have rest in time of spiritual struggle do not obey him.

It is in fact a call for laziness and slackening. But God's children rejoice in labor and even take pride in it (1 Cor. 15:10) and as St. Paul says, *"...in labors more abundant, in stripes above measure, ...in weariness and toil, in sleeplessness often..."* (2 Cor. 11:23-27). He says also, *"Every man shall receive his own reward according to his own labor..."* (1 Cor. 3:8).

Since you know this deceit of the devil, labour for God's sake as much as you are able.

Know that the devil's advice for you to have rest is not faithful advice, nor is it honest, nor is it true. St. Paul of Tammoh tired himself in asceticism till our Lord Jesus Christ appeared to him saying, *'Leave off labor, my beloved Paul.'* But the saint replied, *'What is my labor compared to all your labors, O Lord, for our salvation!'*

It is better for you to weary yourself here on earth and attain crowns for struggling than to have rest here and be exhausted in eternity.

Know that your labor here is not forgotten by God because, *"God is not unjust to forget your work and labor of love."* (Heb. 6:10). Any labor you pass through here is stored for you in eternity.

Here is not a place of rest but a place of struggle and labor.

Thus, when one dies, they say that he reposed i.e. took rest. The devil is not honest in calling you to rest; he deceives you.
He talks to you about looking after your health in the time of asceticism and not when your life is already sinful.

When you fast, the devil in order to deceive you, offers you medical advice, lecturing you on the importance of animal protein and the main amino acids, showing his concern for your body and its health.

But he does not talk about your health if you keep smoking, drinking or practicing youthful lusts which can destroy your health because he is not honest when suggesting to you to take care of your health.

So, if he fights you with the comfort and health of the body, say, *"It is no time for this."* If the war of comfort is of the devil, the war of laziness is a more severe war.

When we are tired in the body, we feel comfort in our souls and vice versa.

When we fulfill our duties, we feel comfort and joy however tired our bodies may be. Also, overcoming our bodies in fasting, watchfulness, kneeling down in worship or in chastity gives us indescribable comfort.

CHAPTER 3

THE INTRIGUES OF THE DEVIL

"...save us from the temptations of the enemy and defeat all his traps set against us."

(From the Eleventh Hour Prayer)

How abundant are the intrigues of the devil! They have no end. If one fails, he changes to use another, then a second, a third and so on until he achieves his purpose. He has no definite plan to attain his goal but takes what he deems suitable for every situation without being restricted by anything.

However, there are among his well-known and obviously repeated plans some methods which have become well-known and recognised:

1. Sin hidden in the guise of virtue.

How easy it is for the devil to offer you some sins under different names, in a style that can be easily accepted so that sins become disguised as virtue.

As the Lord has said, they *"...come to you in sheep's clothing, but inwardly they are ravenous wolves."* (Matt. 7:15)

Mocking or sneering at people is introduced as gentleness and courteousness, affection, familiarity, wittiness and an attempt at humour.

He labels cunning as intelligence!

He offers you harsh treatment of your children and young

brothers under the name of discipline, good-breeding and correction. He even makes your conscience blame you if you do not do so.

He also tries to sell you sin and wrongdoing by giving them enticing names, marketing them very attractively.

The devil does not introduce the sin as sin but conceals it, otherwise a person would refuse it. He gives it another name while it remains the same sin, without any actual change.

He says, *'I shall fight so-and-so with false marketing and make him fall into what I want, perhaps without being aware - or he may be aware but his conscience will not blame him.'*

'If I offer him hypocrisy under this hateful name, he will not accept it. What shall I then do? I shall offer it to him completely concealed – it indeed appears beautiful on the outside (Matt. 23:27) but it is completely different inwardly. I shall give hypocrisy an acceptable name; let it be disguised as keeping others from stumbling, or call it a good example for others.'

It is not wise for the devil to call the sin by its name, as his plans would be revealed and his goal would then be impossible to achieve.

The Lord said to His disciples, **"The time is coming that whoever kills you will think that he offers God service,"** (John 16:2).

Certainly, the devil presented murder to those people as 'zeal' or 'defending religion', 'holy struggle' or 'purifying the earth from sinners'. This might have been the feeling of the scribes, the Pharisees and the elders when they presented the Lord Jesus Christ to be crucified.

Those who rebuked the children and forbade them from going to Christ (Luke 18:15) did not consider this cruelty or indifference towards them but their behavior was clothed as virtue, whether that virtue be 'keeping discipline' or 'regarding the dignity of the good master'.

The devil can also offer lies under the name of 'wisdom'!

He offers them as a kind of good conduct, or as a means of making difficult situations 'easier to deal with'. A physician may tell the patient many lies, putting their own conscience at ease by justifying it as keeping up the patient's morale and protecting him from emotional pain so that the treatment may go more smoothly.

Some people call certain lies 'white lies' and on the first of April they call these lies jests, jokes or other similar names.

In this way, how easy it is for the devil to call dancing an art!

How easy is it for him to call provocative and shameless pictures or statues art. Acting in the theatre and cinema is included under this name 'art', however sinful it may be. Singing or music is also called art, though it may be a cause for temptation and may excite the individual in a way which is not appropriate for a child of God.

Under the name 'art' the devil conceals a large collection of sins and stumbling blocks which do not deserve that beautiful name!

Hiding sin under the guise of virtue is a cunning wile of the devil.

Do you imagine that the devil calls avarice by its name? No one would accept it in this form. He may call it 'good economy', 'saving money for future needs', 'thriftiness' or 'non- extravagance'. If the devil wants to prevent a rich person from giving something to the poor, he will say to him, *"It is not good to accustom them to begging, vagrancy and dependency. Avoiding financially supporting these people is 'wisdom' as it will make them search for work, which will allow them to eat bread by the sweat of their brows, according to the commandment of the Lord God,"* (Gen. 3:19).

Giving sin the name of virtue makes it easier for people to continue doing it...

Not only does this deceit stop people's conscience from rebuking them with respect to the past but it also leads them to continued practice of the same sin in the future.

Would the devil have called the ideas of Arius, Macdonius, Sabilius and others heresies?

No, he convinced them that their heresies were defending the right faith! He provided them with the wrong interpretation of verses in the Holy Bible in order that they might accept his thoughts and convince others of them as well.

Beware then of false advertising and do not allow the devil to deceive you; for sin is sin whatever other name it may go by.

2. Destroying one virtue to gain another.

The devil gets annoyed with your stable virtues, those that have become part of your nature. He tries to destroy them by every means, the easiest of these being the offer of a new virtue. If you practice the new virtue without discernment - for lack of experience - you will lose the first stable virtue. Here are a few examples of this:

i) A person leading a life of meekness, quietness, calmness, peace of heart and decent behaviour.

The devil wants to make this person lose all his gentleness, good words and humility of heart. What can he do? Of course he cannot abuse the person's meekness nor say to him, *"Leave your meek nature which is loved by all..."* but rather he achieves this by displacement. He offers another virtue without saying that it is a substitute. How?

First, he explains to the person the importance of the verse, "Zeal for your house has eaten me up,..." (Ps. 69:9).

He tells him that this was said by King David, who was known for his meekness (Ps. 131:1). He calls to mind that the disciples remembered these words when the Lord Jesus Christ, the meek, *"...had made a whip of cords, ... drove them all out of the temple, with the sheep and the oxen, and poured out the changers' money and overturned the tables..."* (John 2:15-17) and said to them, *"It is written, 'My house shall be called a house of prayer,' but you have made it a 'den of thieves'."* (Matt. 21:13)

He even calls the individual to fight against the faults of

others and provides him with all the necessary verses.

He tells them that the Lord Jesus Christ severely rebuked the Scribes and Pharisees in a whole chapter of the Bible, saying, *"Woe to you, scribes and Pharisees, hypocrites!"* (Matt. 23). He confronted them with all their faults, calling them - more than once – 'blind guides' and saying to them, *"For you are like whitewashed tombs which indeed appear beautiful outwardly,..."* and, *"See! Your house is left to you desolate,..."* (Matt 23:27, 38). John the Baptist also reproved the leaders of the Jews in his days saying, *"Brood of vipers! Who warned you to flee from the wrath to come?"* (Matt. 3:7)

The devil says to this person then; *"Hearken to the words of St. Paul the Apostle who* **commands you to,** *"Convince, rebuke, exhort,..."* (2 Tim. 4:2)" but he does not complete the verse which says, *"...with all longsuffering and doctrine,..."* (2 Tim. 4:2). He does not tell them that these words were said to St. Timothy (the Bishop of Ephesus at the time) and not to everyone. He does not explain to him how St. Paul himself used to reprove, or to say to the priests of Ephesus, *"I did not cease to warn everyone night and day with tears,..."* (Acts 20:31). In this manner, the devil presses so that such a person may reprove and rebuke others, **as if they were Christ, John the Baptist, St. Paul or Timothy the bishop.**

The poor victim is then convinced they should go on reproving everyone around them, not knowing the spiritual way to do so, nor who should reprove whom, nor what his authority to do so is! While reproving others, they fall into the sin of judgment, condemning others in anger, cruelty and defamation. The image of people becomes 'black' in their eyes and perhaps cause many to leave the church because of their conduct. They become a bomb which casts its shrapnel everywhere!

In that way, they lose their meekness, gentleness and decency; they hate people and become hated by them.

They soon get weary of that conduct which does not conform with their nature and try to return to their first condition but they will find their heart to be a different heart and their thoughts are no longer the same. They find that they have lost their simplicity, purity of heart and mind, as well as their good relations with others and they are no longer able to be a good example, which is of benefit to others.

The devil has lured him with a virtue that they misunderstood and made them lose their previous virtue.

They did not keep the original virtue nor gain a new one but instead fell into confusion!

The devil allows him to practice the new 'virtue' because it is not firmly rooted in him and it shall not annoy the devil, for he can shake him easily from it.

Hence, our fathers used to advise their children, saying, '*Refuse any virtue which the devils offer with the intention of destroying another virtue which you have, and say to them, "**This virtue is good but for the sake of God I do not want it.**"*

Indeed, any work that is truly from God does not destroy another work of God. Everyone has his own personality which differs from that of others. What fits one may not fit another. Neither has everyone the authority to arrange and organise, to reprove and rebuke, or to judge and condemn. Whoever is given this authority by God is certainly also given the way to use it properly without doing wrong.

Not everyone can say, *"Woe unto me if I preach not the Gospel."* These words are said by St. Paul who explained the reason for this; *"Necessity is laid upon me,"* and, *"I have been entrusted with a stewardship."* (1 Cor. 9:16-17) but for you, what is the necessity laid upon you? Who committed unto you a dispensation as St. Paul had one committed to him by Christ Himself. John the Baptist had a mission which was given through the announcement of the angel to his father (Luke 1:15-17). St Timothy had a responsibility bestowed upon him through the laying of hands (2 Tim. 1:6)?

ii) A person who lives in purity of heart away from carnal offences.

He lives entirely on guard; he does not read anything which may cause him to stumble. He neither looks at any offensive images nor associates with any persons who may cause him to stumble, nor listens to offensive speech. Thus he keeps his thoughts pure and nothing unholy enters his heart. The devil wants to fight this chaste person but cannot offer him a visible stumbling block because he would surely refuse it. What is it then that he will do?

He opens up the way for him to become a spiritual guide to youth seeking chastity.

He, the devil, argues with him that he should not live in chastity silently, leaving the poor youth to fall everyday into the sin of impurity without offering them sound advice which may save them from their tribulation. The devil tells him to hearken to the advice of the Apostle, *"He who turns a sinner from the error of his way will save a soul from death and cover a multitude of sins,..."* (Jam. 5:20). He goes on convincing him to accept this vital spiritual service until he is convinced and agrees to guide those who come to him. Then comes the next step where he ensnares the servant. He convinces him that **in order that his guidance be practical, he ought to listen to their problems and faults.** They proceed to fill his ears with the tales of their failings, which may include details that may be offensive. The chaste guide is now subject to and listens to what he used to avoid - he becomes acquainted with what he never wanted to know; what he tried to avoid. Now he fills his ears with these words without guilt and he becomes filled with new 'images' of various different types of sin.

By his guidance, the man finds his mind filled with foul images.

He comes to know things which spoil the purity of his mind and defile him with news and tales which, *"...it is shameful even to speak of,..."* (Eph. 5:12). Even if they do not offend him or arouse sinful emotions within him, they would at least defile his mind, like the strange fruit that grew on the tree of the knowledge of good and evil.

If the man tries to leave the service, the devil would say to him, 'And what about those youth?'

They might have become attached to him and found comfort in his guidance. They might trouble his conscience by telling him that they would return to their sins if he left them and they might insist that he go on supporting them. Thus, what happened to Lot the righteous would happen to him; *"...for that righteous man, dwelling among them, tormented his righteous soul from day to day by seeing and hearing their lawless deeds,..."* (2 Pet. 2:8). Our brother here may be vexing himself with hearing only and not seeing, yet what he hears may fill his mind with scenes which will seem to be reality – scenes which he may have never witnessed.

Eventually, this guide will fall, even if it may only be in his thoughts and heart!

He should have, from the beginning, sent for a spiritual father who would have relieved him of this task. He accepted it in good faith, not knowing the outcome of his involvement, not realizing the outcome which the devil had planned for him.

He may eventually succeed in referring them to a spiritual father, however it is too little, too late, for his mind has now stored many tales and images which have destroyed his initial state of purity and placed foreign knowledge in his mind. The type of knowledge of which Solomon the wise said, *"... he who increases knowledge increases sorrow,.."* (Eccl. 1:18).

iii) The wiles of the devil may come in other forms to those in a position of guidance, where rather than offering news or stories which defile the heart, he offers doubts which trouble the mind.

The heart of the person in a position of guidance may be one which is simple in its faith – he reads nothing but that which is spiritual and that which will deepen his attachment to God; not that which will give him an academic understanding of God. He is then asked for guidance by someone with respect to certain doubts which trouble him. These doubts may be complex and require research and study so that solutions are found – something the guide may never have thought of in his simplicity. Gradually, the guide's idea with regard to his faith shifts from a connection at the level of the heart to an understanding of the mind. Only a few have the gift to be able to balance both. Thus the man who is simple by nature finds himself presented with doubts regarding his beliefs which he is not able to refute in the limited scope afforded by his limited mind.

We must know that NOT everyone is qualified to guide those around them.

Those who have such a talent are not wounded by listening to spiritual problems, hearing carnal sins, or problems pertaining to beliefs or doubts with regard to their belief.

In such a case, the resourcefulness of the devil lies in that;

He offers the service of guidance to persons who do not have the talent for it and who may be injured by it.

The devil persists in offering such a service so as to make those persons feel that it is an urgent necessity and a holy duty, warning them in the following manner; *"Therefore, to him who knows to do good and does not do it, to him it is sin,..."* (Jam. 4:17). However, it should be easy to say in humility, *"I do not know much regarding this situation or sin. I was not able to guide myself – therefore, how can I guide others?"*

iv) The devil may offer you a spiritual work by which he eliminates the positive impact of another spiritual work.

When he finds someone offering a deep spiritual prayer and pouring himself before God in heartfelt contemplation, he may send him a person to ask him to make peace between some quarrelling people. As he sits with them trying to reconcile them and hearing the noise, the fuss, the quarrelling and harsh reproach, the effect of prayer and contemplation fades away. This person returns home with nothing in his mind but the heated discussion, which may very well lead him to becoming absent-minded while praying. Such situations require both prayer and spiritual preparation.

The devil may find your prayer full of contemplation, so he wants to distract you.

What would he do? While you are praying, he says to you, *'This is a wonderful and deep contemplation. If others hear it, they will benefit from it. Rise now and write it down lest you should forget it.'* Thus, he takes you away from your prayers in order to write and ends your solemn standing before God in order to sit, write and become interested in others, rather than being interested in standing in the presence of God.

Regarding all virtues that the devil attracts you to, his sole aim is;

To make you lose what you have and/or alluring you with virtues you do not yet have. The devil makes you lose what is already in your hand for the sake of things promised, which may not be achieved, or allows you some virtues then steals them away from you in due time.

3. Using virtues out of their place.

The Holy Bible says, *"To everything there is a season, a time for every purpose under heaven,..."* (Eccl. 3:1). If virtues are used out of place or not in their due time, they may lead to an adverse result and will not serve their spiritual purpose. Here are some of the various intrigues of the devil regarding this specific type of warfare.

During times of repentance, in which penitence is required, the devil offers the virtue of joy.

He reminds you of all the verses related to joy so that repentance, penitence and tears may be lost, knowing that they are necessary for proceeding in the life of repentance. At the same time, he conceals other verses such as, *"Blessed are those who mourn, for they shall be comforted,..."* (Matt. 5:4).

In this way, the devil uses the method of the 'single verse'.

The Lord Jesus Christ refused this method. When the devil addressed Him on the mount, *"...for it is written..."* the Lord answered, *"It is written again..."* (Matt. 4:6-7).

Thus, He showed us that the method of the single verse used by the devil cannot lead to a proper spiritual understanding, since there are other verses which further explain the subject matter of the single verse quoted.

The devil may also use various verses of a certain type to serve his purpose.

He feeds us the verses pertaining to mercy when firmness is required and where punishment is necessary; he feeds us the verses pertaining to punishment where forgiveness, compassion and mercy are required.

The devil tries to convince a person to be silent, offering various verses of the Holy Bible on silence at times when speech and action are required. In contradiction to this, he offers verses regarding the advantages and importance of talking when it is wiser to remain silent.

The devil may give a person some verses which do not fit his character or position but are suitable for others.

For example, he deceives a layman by feeding him verses which concern the Apostles and clergyman alone and do not fit him, which may cause him to 'follow' with unfounded stubbornness the words of the Lord Jesus Christ to His twelve disciples, *"Do not call anyone on earth your father..."* (Matt. 23:9).

Another example is a violent person who, whenever he meets anyone doing something wrong, he strikes them! His reason being the misuse of the verse, *"Early I will destroy all the wicked of the land, that I may cut off all the evildoers from the city of the LORD..."* (Ps. 101:8) – an idea fed to him by the devil.

4. Planting suspicion.

The devil plants suspicion in every area of spiritual life, as a suspicious person is usually weak and can easily be conquered by the devil.

For example, the devil plants doubts with respect to repentance. These doubts will be either with the possibility of repentance or its acceptance by God.

He suggests to the person that it is not easy for him to remove such sins which have become a part of his character, are part of his habits or have become so loved by him that he can never go without them. Filling that person with doubts concerning his ability, the devil conceals completely God's ability to help him overcome his sins, or makes him doubt it as David the prophet said, *"LORD, how they have increased who trouble me! Many are they who rise up against me. Many are they who say of me, "There is no help for him in God..."* (Ps. 3:2). Then if the person insists on repentance, the devil makes them doubt God's acceptance of their repentance, either because it came at a late stage or because it is not true repentance or because his sins are so dreadful that they cannot be forgiven easily but need punishment beyond what a person is able to bear!

The objective of the devil by all this is to throw the repentant into despair.

This would make him lose heart and lead him to continue in sin.

The devil may also make him doubt God's mercy, giving him countless verses about God's justice and punishment in cases in which perhaps the punishments mentioned are for sins far lighter than theirs.

The devil uses suspicion to overthrow the individual's personal life also.

He plants doubt concerning which path of life is preferable, celibacy or marriage.

No matter which path is chosen, he makes a person doubt. If the person chooses celibacy, the devil makes them doubt whether they can lead such a life or not and shows them that it is a very hard way, which fits only those, *"...to whom it has been given,"* (Matt. 19:11) and that, *"... each one has his own gift from God..."* (1 Cor. 7:7).

The devil asks, *'How do you know that this is your gift?'* and shows him the failures of some holy people and says, *"Are you better than David and Samson, they who had the Spirit of the Lord?"*

On the other hand, if the person chooses marriage, the devil says to him, *"You have lost the crown of virginity."* He puts before him the words of St. Paul the Apostle, *"He who is unmarried cares for the things of the Lord; how he may please the Lord. But he who is married cares about the things of the world; how he may please his wife.,"* (1 Cor. 7:32-33) and *"He who does not give her [a virgin] in marriage does better."* (1 Cor. 7:38).

Thus, he leaves him in confusion, not knowing which way to choose!

The devil also plants doubts with respect to seclusion and ministry.

If a person chooses the way of seclusion, the devil describes to him the glories of ministry. He demonstrates how it is the way of the Apostles and heroes of faith, *"...who turn many to righteousness like the stars forever and ever,"* (Dan. 12:3); and *"Nor do they light a lamp and put it under a basket, but on a lampstand, and it gives light to all who are in the house.* **Let your light so shine before men**, *that they may see your good works and glorify your Father in heaven."* (Matt. 5:15-16).

However, if the person chooses the way of ministry, the devil says to him, *"You have lost the way of the angels who are on earth, lost the life of quietude and calmness in which one is devoted to God alone. You have chosen the way of Martha, whom the Lord reproved with the words, "Thou art careful and troubled about many things."* (Luke 10:41-42).' The devil emphasizes that the person did not choose the way of Mary, who sat at Jesus's feet and *"...has chosen the good part..."* (Luke 10:42). He reminds him also of the vision in which St. Arsenius the secluded hermit appeared better than St. Moses the Black, who loved and served the brethren.

Thus, the devil goes on planting doubts as St. John Climacus says, *"The devil fights the monk who lives in seclusion with the love and service of the brethren. But he fights the monk who serves the brethren in society with the love of seclusion and the life of peace, prayers and contemplation."*

The devil plants suspicion in social relations as a whole.

He plants suspicions between husband and wife, between friends, partners in business and between bosses and subordinates. He makes one person doubt the love of the other, or doubt his faithfulness and honesty. He plants suspicions regarding the behaviour of people and their intentions and purposes. The devil does all this to shake relations among people, lead them into discord and disputes and destroy the love upon which humanity's spiritual and social lives depend.

Even simple matters are complicated by the devil's various intrigues – it is very possible for him to make any simple problem into a complex and longstanding issue!

The devil plants doubts in the matter of faith and belief.

All the heresies and schisms which humanity has suffered are the making of the devil and his thoughts. All the various conflicting denominations and sects of Christianity as well as atheism were all caused by the devil.

The devil also makes people doubt the possibility of life with God.

He explains that the spiritual life is difficult or impossible; for who can go along the difficult way, or enter through the narrow gate (Matt. 7:13-14)? Who can attain the life of perfection which the Lord requires from us (Matt. 5:48) and who can escape the wars of the devils?

In all this, he conceals the role of Grace and the work of the Holy Spirit in man's salvation and conceals the abundant assistance of God!

The devil may plant doubts in one's heart concerning their father confessor.

He makes the person doubt the father confessor's concern and love for him. He makes him doubt whether he will keep his secrets. He puts suspicions in his mind concerning the father confessor's guidance and whether it is correct and fit for spiritual growth or not - and concerning his knowledge and spirituality. The devil wants to separate, by any and all means, his prey from their father confessor, who reveals to him the wars of the devils, their intrigues and their cunning. Thus the poor person remains without a guide and becomes easy prey for the devils.

The devil makes the person doubt his father confessor in order to push the person towards disobeying him, leaving him or concealing his disposition from him; things which are all wrong. He may even make him doubt the sacrament of confession itself, saying to him, '*Why would you confess to a human being like yourself?*'

He may make a person doubt virtue itself.

For example, he would say to him, "*What is the need for humility and meekness? They weaken your personality! What does it mean that you leave your own rights instead of getting it by force, thus letting others deceive you?*" The devil carries out the same thing with the other virtues.

As for you, you must not accept such suspicions, and whenever you feel suspicious say, "*This is the work of the devil.*"

Do not accept any suspicions within you, nor be doubtful, nor let doubts fester and grow.

If it is possible for you to discuss a certain doubt, do so and reveal its falsity, or pray to God to remove it from you and remember the words of the Holy Bible, *"...be steadfast, immovable,"* (1 Cor. 15:58).

5. The war of despair.

Despair is a weapon which the devil uses after lengthy and thorough preparation.

These preparations may be successive falls in which the devil traps his prey unceasingly until the prey cries out at last, *"There is no hope for me. It is impossible to be saved as long as I am in this state!"*

The devils' preparations may also be suggestions which the he puts continuously inside his prey under the pretext of humility! He repeats every day, *"I am weak and helpless, I am all sin."* However, instead of being led by this to humility to repentance, he becomes weak in spirit and feels that he is not able to rise.

The beginning of the war of despair may be a great fall (such as that of Judas the Disciple) by which the devil makes one feel that forgiveness is not possible.

The devil is very experienced in enlarging faults so as to throw the person who commits them into despair.

The devil is very cunning in this respect. Before the fall, the person commits a sin which appears to be 'normal' and 'expected'; it is justified through the cunning of the devil. After the sin is committed, the devil either continues in the same manner, presenting the sin as 'easy', so that the person might repeat it, or he exaggerates the gravity of the sin in order to lead the person to despair. He says to the person, *"Is it possible for God to forgive such a sin?"*

The sinner may be made to feel that he has fallen into blaspheming the Holy Spirit!

Thus, he feels that he will have no forgiveness (Mark 3:29), although the sin cannot in fact be considered as blasphemy against the Holy Spirit. Hence, the devil may cause the individual to dismiss the Holy Spirit (or feel a supposed dismissal of the Holy Spirit) entirely from their heart. Thus, the person does not repent and accordingly is not forgiven, as forgiveness depends on repentance and repentance depends on the work of the Holy Spirit in the heart – this is not possible if the heart has dismissed the Holy Spirit or feels as if the Holy Spirit has left them.

The devil may lead the person to despair, making them feel that their repentance cannot be accepted!

He says to them, *"You wish to stop this sin? It is impossible!! Sin now runs in your blood. Your resolution is over, and your will has broken - even the wish to repent does not exist now. How many times did you try to repent and failed to do so? How many times did you confess your sins and return to commit them, perhaps to a greater extent?"* So the devil bombards the person till they yield to this harassment and stops struggling.

The devil then says, *"You are entirely in my hands. I can move you, as I wish. There is no need for you struggle against me - you will fail and gain nothing by it."*

Of course, your fears have no basis and his threats are false.

God is able to give man repentance no matter how severe his condition may be. History tells us of the once sinful lives of St. Mary the Egyptian, St. Pelagia, St. Augustine and St. Moses the Black – individuals we consider as saints today in our churches.

Whenever a person falls, the devil tries to throw them into despair.

He convinces them that their fall is not temporary, but everlasting.

How wonderful are the comforting words in the Book of Micah the prophet, *"Do not rejoice over me, my enemy; when I fall, I will arise,"* (Mic. 7:8) and *"For a righteous man may fall seven times and rise again,..."* (Prov. 24:16). Note how in spite of the repeated falls, the Holy Bible calls the man who rises again *"...righteous..."*.

Among the means which lead to despair are the devil's attacks during our times of greater spirituality.

This is one of most famous intrigues of the devil – one which has become well-known to us. To be able to understand this intrigue, let us consider the following situation:

You spend a spiritual night in church, at the beginning of a new year, full of desire and determination to start a holy, blessed year. You attend the Liturgy and partake of Holy Communion, then you go out of the church - only to meet a troublesome fellow whom the devil sends to you to disturb and aggravate you. You get angry and sin; here the devil strikes you with despair and you say, *"How could I fall after all this? There was no point to this night spent in the church!"*

If this happens, do not despair. It is a well-known attack of his.

Say with the prophet, *"When I fall, I shall rise."* (Mic. 7:8). Know that the devil will not diminish his warfare. At the beginning of every New Year, on every spiritual day, after every prayer, at the beginning of each and after every time we partake of Holy Communion, expect a blow from him. If he strikes, say to him, *"Seek another game; your tricks are now well-known to me."*

Believe me, the wars during spiritual occasions are countless but know that they are merely a result of the envy of the devil, who seeks to hinder any spiritual work or success.

Among the means by which the devil leads us to despair is by attracting us to carry out a spiritual canon that is at a higher level than we can bear.

He gives a person 'right-hand blows', convincing him to aim for high levels of spirituality that he cannot attain; encouraging him with all his power. If the father confessor advises him to advance gradually, trying to direct him towards a more achievable target, the devil convinces him to become suspicious of his father confessor and leads him to question the fathers' spirituality.

It is easy for a person to stay at a high level for two or three days without a good foundation but after this he cannot go on and finds himself to be failing the task he has set for himself. Here the devil starts to reproach him and throws him into despair, saying, *"You are not fit for the spiritual path! Your nature does not allow you to live a proper spiritual life."*

The devil goes on breaking him apart. However, if that person had advanced gradually, in accordance with the advice of his father confessor, he would have eventually attained the level which the devil was forcing him to start at.

The devil was able to convince the scribes and Pharisees to behave according to this manner.

In giving spiritual guidance they would *"...bind heavy burdens, hard to bear, and lay them on men's shoulders; but they themselves will not move them with one of their fingers."* (Matt. 23:4). These heavy burdens may sometimes lead people to despair, for the person who carries them may say, *'Who can bear this? Who may be saved?'*

But the holy Apostles did not behave like this.

In accepting the nations into the faith, they decided, *"...we should not trouble those from among the Gentiles who are turning to God."* (Acts 15:19). They sent to them the words of comfort, *"For it seemed good to the Holy Spirit, and to us, to lay upon you no greater burden than these necessary things."* (Acts 15:28). St. Paul the Apostle also said, *"I fed you with milk and not with solid food; for until now you were not able to receive it, and even now you are still not able,..."* (1 Cor. 3:2).

So, if the devil tempts you with things above your level, do not accept them.

Say to him, *"Get thee hence, Satan. I have my spiritual guide, whom I obey. You do not intend any good for me. You have your own ways which are improper and do not lead to the right end. It is said of St. Anthony that the devil awakened him one night to pray, but he refused the advice, saying to him, "I pray whenever I want and will not obey what you say.""*

The devil lifts a person up in order to overthrow him and when he falls, the devil leads him into despair with all of his malevolence. Fighting with the weapon of despair is a key tool implemented by the devil because:

When a person gets desperate they become easily broken. They lose self-confidence and faith in God. They no longer believe it is possible to lead a spiritual life – they believe they have ultimately failed.

This is what the devil wants; for there to be no resistance from his prey so that they may ultimately be destroyed. It is as if the devil is saying to the person who yields to him, *"You will not escape from my grasp. You will certainly go to hell. There is no use. I advise you to enjoy the world so as to avoid losing both this present life and the one to come!"*

The devil convinces such a person of the difficulty of spiritual life and exaggerates their weak and corrupt nature! He convinces them that they will not be able to escape from his grasp nor from divine justice.

This is the ultimate aim of the devil when he begins his war of despair. Yet there is a simple response we can use to combat this warfare: we do not fight with our own wills - *"...for the battle is the Lord's..."* (1 Sam. 17:47) and He causes us to triumph in Christ (2 Cor. 2:14). Though we ourselves are not able to do anything because of our weakness and corruption and because of the difficulty of the way; yet we can do all things through Christ who strengthens us (Phil. 4:13). We are supported by the work of Grace, the power of the Holy Spirit who is in us, by the angels sent to minister to us (Heb. 1:14) and we are further supported by the intercession of the saints.

As for the devil, he has no power over us, and we should not fear his threats. How true are the words of the Apostle, *"Resist the devil and he will flee from you,..."* (Jam. 4:7). Divine justice was achieved by the Lord upon the cross when he granted us, out of His great love, glorious salvation (Heb. 2:3).

Ultimately, *"If we confess our sins, He is faithful and just to forgive us our sins and to cleanse us from all unrighteousness."* (1 John 1:9). He shall wash us and we shall be whiter than snow (Ps. 50:7) as He has said to us, *"Though your sins are like scarlet, they shall be as white as snow..."* (Is. 1:18).

In contrast to the way the devil fights with despair, **the Holy Bible encourages us and gives us hope, which is one of the greatest virtues** (1 Cor. 13:13).

Many are God's promises to us and to the church; *"The gates of Hades shall not prevail against it,..."* (Matt. 16:18), *"We are kept by the power of God..." (*1 Pet. 1:5), we are inscribed upon the palms of His hands (Is. 49:16) etc. The Holy Bible also says, *"For God has not given us a spirit of fear, but of power ...."* (2 Tim. 1:7). Thus, the Apostle advises us more than once not to lose heart (2 Cor. 4:1, 16), (Gal. 6:9).

If you are going along the spiritual path and you fall, do not think that you cannot continue, or become despondent, but

rise up and proceed on the way.

The devil envies your progress and seeks to hinder it. Do not let his obstacles lead you to despair. On the contrary, rise with greater vigour and know that if you were not successful in your spiritual work, the devil would not fight you! Indeed, why should the devil tire himself in fighting a person who is already failing? He attacks a person who is steadfast in the way, who is able to resist him and whose resistance he fears.

Hearken then to the words of the Apostle, *"...be steadfast, immovable..."* (1 Cor. 15:58).

Be courageous in the Lord and do not lose hope.

Do not become despondent, no matter how powerful the wars of the devil are.

Do not become despondent. No matter how many times you fall or if you have forgotten the commandments and failed to practice them.

Do not become despondent if at the beginning you are weak or unsuccessful.

Say to yourself, *"All these are simple wars – I shall cleave to God. I shall go along the way to God even if I do it begrudgingly. Even if I fall a hundred times on the way, I shall rise. I shall never accept despair because it is from the devil."*

6. The devil changes up his plans.

The devil does not stick to a certain plan when fighting man. It is a simple matter for him to change his behaviour and his plans if it will allow him to overthrow an individual in an easier manner.

We shall now give some examples:

i) The devil violently fights a certain youth with adultery, tiring him out and eventually causing him to fall. The youth then begins a life of repentance and becomes more focused on guarding himself against this specific sin; keeping away from its causes, closing all potential openings by which it can attack him (whether it be visually, audibly or via specific social interactions) and at the same time strengthening himself from within by spiritual practices, the mother of these being heartfelt repentance in prayer.

What is the devil able to do against such strong caution? He says; *"I shall leave him now. I shall not fight him with this sin for a long time until he thinks that he has overcome it completely and becomes less cautious against it; instead I shall fight him with another sin."*

He leaves him for a year, two years, or possibly three years without fighting him with this particular sin, without placing any stumbling blocks and without feeding him any thoughts but he will make the individual fall into other sins, such as pride.

The poor youth, seeing that he is saved from adultery, rejoices, and may be easily tempted by the devil into thinking himself able to apply a higher level of fasting, Bible reading and service. While his mind no longer recalls his weakness and he becomes satisfied with his spiritual course, the devil calls him to teach others to attain his same level. He shows them that the others are negligent in their spiritual life and that he has far surpassed them – he then falls into the sin of pride.

The devil also calls him to reprove, rebuke and condemn them, saying, *"Your father does not pray, your mother does not fast, your brothers do not partake of Holy Communion, your family does not read the Holy Bible. Go and reprove them violently."*

This reproof leads the individual to despising others for straying from God - the heart becomes great in its own eyes. As the person attempts to gather up the tare, he himself becomes a tare. Under the name of righteousness, he begins to insult, speak in anger, condemn, despise others and become arrogant. He becomes cloaked in his own vanity and pride, saying like the Pharisee, *"God, I thank You that I am not like other men; extortioners, unjust, adulterers..."* (Luke 18:11).

The devil thinks, *"Whoever perishes through pride is like him that perishes through adultery. Both will perish."*

Is not death by tuberculosis the same as death as a result of cancer? The cause may vary but the outcome desired by the devil is achieved.

As for the sin of adultery, which the youth thinks he has escaped from, it will return to him one day, only at a point when he is less cautious, less prudent and his resistance has faltered. At that time, the devil will strike him in such a way that he is not able to regain control of himself. When you ask the devil how he achieved this, he answers:

"During the time in which the youth was not attacked by the war of adultery, he thought it would not be possible for it to fight him again and that it no longer had a place in his life. He was convinced that it was one of those sins that only fights' beginners and thus it was impossible that it would fight him! Many even began to seek his guidance in learning to resist such a sin."

Thus, he willingly allows himself to be exposed to details and instances of the sin which, beforehand, he was on guard against. He may further begin to reads books on the subject matter, which he had previously protected himself against, in order to answer the questions of those who come to him for guidance. His mind becomes filled with thoughts which leave within him certain impressions that subtly, and without his realising, affect him negatively. By this point, Grace has abandoned him as a result of his prideful condemnation of others. At this stage, the devil strikes him with the sin of adultery and it easily overthrows him. The plan of the devil succeeded, although there was a change of course along the way.

The devil now says with glee, *"I relieved him from that sin for some time so that he was no longer prepared for it and was not guarded against it. Now he will indulge in this sin and the thoughts I shall give him. During this period of slackening and indulgence which has come, I shall fight him with the sin which he has forgotten for years and he shall fall continuously without resistance."*

This is the nature of the devil! He will not fight you with a certain sin for a time not out of his mercy or his despondency but out of his malice, for he is preparing a different trap for you.

ii) Another example.
If a person who falls in committing sins of the tongue and behavior, such as anger, condemning others, insulting others and uttering abusive words, 'awakens' and begins to deeply practice silence in order to control and mitigate these sins. What does the devil do in order to overthrow such a person?

The devil begins to say, *"Alright, I can modify my plans and instead of fighting him with the sins of the tongue and with anger, I'll fight him with a sin like vanity, for example. The person must become entirely convinced that there is no one better than him. But how? I shall relieve him from the sins of the tongue for now and I will convince him to take a 'leap' in his spiritual life."*

The person begins to think that there is none like him in his asceticism and starts to behave conceitedly, to the extent that he might disagree with and disregard the advice of his father confessor, who objects to his extravagance and vanity. He no longer submits to anyone nor obeys anyone; he does not consult with anyone and does not respect anyone.

Vanity traps him and completely destroys him. The sins of the tongue are no longer even a problem and yet the individual is led to his demise.

However, this is not the end of the story, as his vanity will inevitably cause him to clash with others and will surely cause him to fall in the sins of the tongue without the devil having to tempt him and to a degree which is worse than before!

The devil adapts his plans continuously. He first considers the condition of the person and chooses for him the fall which is most 'suitable' for him. He knows when he should fight, how and with what means.

Whoever does not fall using a certain path will fall by another. Whoever does not fall in a certain sin now will fall in the same sin afterwards. The traps of the devil are both abundant and elaborate.

iii) A third example to show how the devil changes his plans.

Lent begins for another year and the devil is considering how to fight a young man so that he may not fast, noting that the previous year he (the devil) attempted the same thing in vain.

In order to throw the youth into doubt with respect to fasting, he begins by attacking him saying, *"What does it mean to abstain from animal products? Is it not better to abstain from sin and fight the animal which is inside you, for what is the use of fasting without chastity and purity? Is not your fast unacceptable due to your sin?"*

The young man responds, *"I am performing the commandments of the Holy Bible, "These you ought to have done, without leaving the others undone,"* (Matt. 23:23). *So I try my best to fast both bodily and spiritually: abstaining both from food and the lusts of the flesh; "...I discipline my body and bring it into subjection,"* (1 Cor. 9:27) *by depriving my flesh of the foods it loves so that it may learn to be made subject to the spirit."*

The warfare of the devil does not stop at this point; he continues; *"But you are weak and your health cannot endure fasting. You certainly need animal proteins in order to be healthy during this period in which you are still growing."*

The young man retorts with the words that Christ used; *"Man shall not live by bread alone,"* (Matt. 4:4). *"Remember that Adam and Eve lived on fruit and vegetables, then on the herbs of the field (Gen. 1:29, 3:18). The Holy Bible did not mention that they fell ill for lack of animal proteins!"*

The devil continues; *"All right then, you can fast but there is no need to fast from the beginning of Lent for it is far too long. You must also ensure that you do not force yourself to fast more than you can lest the devil should fight you with vain glory! You know the diabolic wars and the danger of the right-hand blows."*

The young man answers; *"I do not want to slacken in my asceticism, for the Lord requires us to be perfect (Matt. 5:48). No matter how much fasting I do, what is it compared to the fasting of the holy people? It is nothing."*

The young man fasted this year, not listening to the advice of the devil. Lent comes around the next year and the youth still insists on fasting.

The devil has found that any attempt to prevent this young man from fasting is in vain, so he changes his course of action. He begins to do the complete opposite of what he was doing previously.

He says to the young man, "*Fasting is so useful! Great benefit comes from the prolonged period of abstinence. You ought to abstain from food until sunset every single day of Lent. But you must first consult your father confessor and get his consent.*" The devil knows that the father confessor would not agree with the youth performing such a difficult labour and now his trap is set.

The father confessor does not agree and calls the young man to advance gradually.

Here the devil finds his opening saying, "*Your father confessor is not experienced in fasting and his guidance will hinder your spiritual growth. You will not advance nor taste the sweetness of fasting. I fear he might even advise you to break your fast during Passion Week! It is better for you to change your father confessor or you should evade consulting your father confessor with regards to the matter of fasting. Leave these matters out and I shall help you to decide what to do.*"

Thus, the devil changed his plan from planting doubts concerning fasting to doubts concerning the father confessor. He does not care for the kind of war he uses; he is solely concerned with ensuring the person falls.

By separating the young man from his spiritual father, he left him without a guide and thus the person acted as he saw fit; a fatal error to make in our spiritual lives. He became filled with the pride of heart by which he thought himself wiser and more prudent than his guide. All this leads to only one possible outcome – the fall of the youth.

iv) A fourth example - the devil of vainglory.

This devil changes his methods continuously to adapt to the conditions that are before him.

This devil is known as the 'round' devil – he is not like a 'cube', which requires a base to stand upon, but he is like a ball which is able to roll in any and all directions.

If you sit at a table and do not partake of the food, he says to you, *"I admire your asceticism. You are not drawn to eat like the others around you."* However, if you eat like those around the table, he says to you, *"In like manner do the saints act; they pretend to eat while they are in fact fasting so as to hide their virtue."*

If you speak and those around you are attentive to what you say, he says, *"It is the voice of wisdom by which you speak that gains the admiration of those who hear you'.* On the other hand if you keep silent, he says, *'Silence is the virtue which saints like St. Arsenius practiced."*

Be wise when dealing with the devil and do not believe what he tells you, nor be affected by his words and judgement. If he fights you with self-praise remember your sins and points of weakness and reprove yourself. Otherwise, remember what it is that you lack in pursuing the life of righteousness to balance out the praise you hear.

If the devil adapts the plans that he uses to make you fall, you should also change the method by which you fight him.

St. John the Short, who was praised by the devils for the virtues he had attained (for all who were in the hermitage used to ask him for a word of benefit), he would answer the devils saying, *"Who is this poor man that you praise? Have I attained what St. Anthony or St. Bemwa attained? I am completely filled with sin."* and when they said to him, *"Indeed you are a sinner and will perish",* he answered, *"Have you forgotten God's love and mercy?"* Due to St John's wisdom in his answers, the devils would say to him, *"You puzzle us. If we lift you up, you humble yourself, and if we humble you, you lift yourself up."* Act likewise in your dealings with the devil.

If the devils praise you, remember your sins. If they relieve you from their wars say to yourself, *"Perhaps they are preparing for me a trap which I cannot yet see. May God have mercy upon me who is a sinner."*

Always remember that you have not yet attained a level of spirituality at which the devils will fight you openly. Remember the brother who complained to St. Bishoy that the devils fought him. The devil appeared to St. Bishoy and said, *"Who is that brother, that I may fight him? I did not even hear that he has become a monk!"*

The real wars of the devils are violent, and perhaps most of us have not been exposed to them. The wars which were fought by the saints were violent. God forbid that we suffer even a fraction of what they did.

7. Depression.

Here, the devil fights in contradiction to the way in which the devil of vainglory fights the person. The devil seeks to exaggerate the feeling of despondency in those who are

repentant, penitent and aware of their sins in order to lead them to perdition.

The devil will cunningly pick a single verse from the Holy Bible and put it before them always in order to make them fall into extreme despair. For example, *"For by a sad countenance the heart is made better..."* (Eccl. 7:3) - or he may remind them that the Bible has no mention of Christ laughing but it mentions several times that He wept.

Whenever one falls in sin or is fought violently with a sin, the devil increases his 'sadness' (or despair) by saying, *"You are not the son of God, for you are a sinner, and the Holy Bible says, "Whoever has been born of God does not sin,..."''* (1 John 3:9, 5:18).

The devil continues, saying, *"You do not deserve to be a child not only of God but of your father confessor. You are a shame to him. You defame him."*

He continues, *"It is better that you leave this righteous father alone lest people should taunt him saying, 'Is this the example set by your spiritual children?'. Leave him lest he should also be condemned because of you and so that you may not grieve him further with the condition he sees you in."*

Thus, the child is turned away from feeling the compassion and fatherhood of God through their alienation from their confession father.

Even when they hold the Holy Bible in order to read it, the devil says to them, *"Do you dare to hold the word of God with your impure hands? Every word condemns you, for the Lord*

Jesus Christ Himself says about you and those similar to you, " The word that I have spoken will judge him in the last day," (John 12:48)." Thus, he fills their soul with sadness till they are forced to leave the Bible, bitter and upset.

If they are servants, he makes them abandon their service, thinking they are undeserving.

The devil says to them, *"Service is for saints and not sinners. You do not deserve to hold the position of a Sunday school teacher, for you will become a stumbling block. The ministry will also make it easy for you to forget your sins, though you must put them before you constantly and grieve for them day and night."*

When they stand to pray, the devil prevents them saying, *"Do not forget that "...the sacrifice [prayer] of the wicked is an abomination to the Lord," (Prov. 15:8, 28:9). Remember the publican who stood afar and would not lift his eyes to heaven (Luke 18:13); you are being unmindful of this account by speaking to God while you are breaking His commandments. You should be ashamed of yourself! Stop this evil prayer!"*

Thus, through despair, the devil leads them away from all means of grace so that he may have no barrier in attacking this individual.

When the devil is alone with this now lonely person; a person who is broken, with no Bible or prayers, no father confessor, no service or church meetings and perhaps with no friends around them (for they might have abandoned them due to their constant sadness) they become easy prey for the devil.

How easy it then becomes for the devil to say to them, *"Leave this religious environment - for this is the cause of your grief!"*

Or rather, how easy it is to spread this idea through relatives, or a physician and to thus attract them gradually to some means of amusement by which they may alleviate their sadness. This is a temporary solution, for there will only be a temporary respite until the devil uses another of his wiles so as to separate them from God completely.

Ultimately the devil will seek to overthrow them with despair, for which sadness prepares the way.

The aim of the devil, in using 'sadness', was to cut off the potential for the person to gain hope or forgiveness.

He removed them far away from remembering the loving God, who received his lost son in joy and jubilation, putting upon him His best gown (Luke 15:22-24). The Lord even says, *"There is joy in the presence of the angels of God over one sinner who repents."* (Luke 15:10). It is true that saints wept for their sins, but not without hope, for the Holy Bible says, *"...least you sorrow as others who have no hope..."* (1 Thess. 4:13).

Sorrow over our sins should not separate us from God but rather bring us nearer to Him and increase our love for him. For in spite of our sins, He forgave us; moreover, He says, *"For I will forgive their iniquity, and their sin I will remember no more..."* (Jer. 31:34). God finds no pleasure in the death of a sinner - He would rather that he returns from his ways and lives (Ezk. 18:23).

The problem of the person who loses hope through sadness is that he follows the counsel of the devil, who is the father of all liars. In contrast, the words of God are full of love and comfort.

Sadness is intended to lead us to humility and penitence, not to despair and separation from God. If the devil succeeds in using sadness through his wicked ways, he will certainly destroy the person who falls into it.

St. Peter the Apostle, after denying Christ, wept bitterly, and the Lord Jesus Christ appeared to him and said, *"Feed My lambs... Tend My sheep."* (John 21:15-16). What more hope is there than this? Thus, a sad countenance which causes the heart to become bitter should not be separated from love and hope.

8. Speed.

The works of the devil are characterised by the speed or haste in which they are performed, in contrast to the works of God which are performed in calmness, deliberation and patience and are executed precisely and in due time. Simply consider the plan of salvation and the carrying out of God's promises to characters of the Old Testament and you will see this to be true.

The devil offers you a thought and pushes you repeatedly so that you may perform what it tells you rapidly.

When the diabolic thought attacks you from within, you are filled with a growing enthusiasm to perform it. You feel a fire burning within and are motivated to carry out the matter immediately without lingering in thought, not allowing yourself time to discuss, examine, evaluate, consider or meditate upon it.

The purpose of this haste is to cause you neither to think nor consult others about the matter.

By the speed of his works he seeks to leave you isolated - without the interference of others, without time for consultation and in the absence of any benefit that can be gained from sound advice, experience and spiritual practice; no friends or relatives, no father confessor or guide. The sole aim is that you carry out the thought quickly.

By his haste, he wants to prevent you from submitting the matter before God in prayer.

He does not want to give you a chance to pray concerning this matter so that you may not seek the response God will give; so that you might not have a chance to raise up prayers in a Liturgy, or to fast in expectation of God's guidance. The thought presses upon you heavily and the devil convinces you that this thought is a fact – that it requires no further discussion. The fathers said concerning this,

"Any thought which presses on you to perform it rapidly is of the devil."

Of course, the thoughts we refer to here are not the 'good ones', i.e. the desire to repent and return to God, or to be attached to Him in love but thoughts which require discussion and do not urgently need to be performed (unlike the thought to save a drowning person or extinguish a fire).

Many times has a person carried out an action rapidly only to regret it and return in repentance. The thoughts of sin and lust that we are plagued with sometimes feel so pressing that the person finds no time to think about it and change their feelings.

Further, the devil uses this 'haste' in order to remain undiscovered.

Perhaps behind the thought or the suggestion which is offered to you there is a wile or intrigue of the devil which he does not want discovered through contemplation, consultation or prayer. So he presses that it be performed quickly before his wile is discovered. Here the advantage of having a father confessor is made apparent in that he reveals the intrigues of the devil. The wisdom of the desert fathers teaches that, *"Those who are without a guide, shall fall like the leaves of the tree."*

The children of God should not obey every thought which comes to mind.

Consider St. Macarius, who, when the thought to go into the wilderness in order to see the anchorites came to him, remained fighting the thought for three years, in order that he might determine whether or not it was from God. How extraordinary this is! Even this great saint did not act quickly in seeking to carry out a thought, although it was, in fact, spiritually edifying.

The saints saw no harm in persevering with their thoughts, only benefit.

They did not carry out any thought rapidly lest it was of the devil. Delaying carrying out the thought gave them a chance both to ensure the thought was not destructive and to wait for God to announce his perfect judgment upon the goodness (or lack thereof) of the thought. They lived by these beautiful words:

"That which is of God is established, and that which is not of God is removed away."

When the devil appeared to St. Galion in the form of a monk, saying that he was one of the roaming anchorites and that his companions were roaming fathers, he allowed them to join him and the devil asked him to walk with him; Saint Galion obeyed the devil without submitting the matter before God or before his father confessor. The devils that appeared to him caused him to become lost in the wilderness and left him in scorn saying, *"You will die here alone, in this wilderness."* Despite this God saved him.

9. Extended and gradual attacks.

The means used by the devil in his wars vary and may appear to contradict one another, yet they all have a single aim – to cause the fall of man. He differs his means according to the circumstances of the individual he is fighting. The devil does not adhere to the same 'pattern of attack' for all, lest people should become accustomed to his wiles.

Sometimes he may strike suddenly and without warning, so that he might catch the person unawares and cause them to fall. At other times, he carries out 'long, gradual advances' (i.e. small, consistent attacks over an extended period of time) so that the person is not conscious of how far the devil

has taken them towards perdition.

Although these gradual advances require an extended period time in order for them to happen, the devil does not care, for if it results in the fall of a child of God then the devil has achieved his aim. This method is used in order to bring down the person who does not accept sin (or specific sins) easily. He leads them to sin gradually, patiently, making only small advancements which will inevitably lead to the demise of the individual.

He achieves his 'target' sin by splitting the sin into stages - establishing and concreting each stage over time.

The first step to the sin may not in fact be sinful at all, nor may it alert the conscience of the individual. The first step which led to the fall of David the prophet was his refraining from going to war. He sent out the army and remained at home. The second step was allowing himself to be spoilt by luxury after having had to wander from one wilderness to another during the period in which King Saul was pursuing him. These stages passed without David the prophet being aware of any fault or wrongdoing.

However, there were certain ideologies which were planted within him subconsciously; these robbed him of his spiritual ardour without his realising.

Then King David reached the third step - his taking of many wives. Although this was allowed at the time, he undoubtedly had fallen to the level of the flesh. Though it was permitted, this was not the perfect system that God created. His flesh had control over him, whether he was aware of it or not.

Soon came the fourth step: he ascended to the roof of his palace to walk about and gaze upon the kingdom he had inherited. He allowed himself to look down at the property of others and see what they desired to keep private - thus began his fall.

The fifth step was the hard blow, by which the devil overthrew the great psalmist into lust, then adultery.

The sixth step was his attempt to conceal his original sin with a succession of other sins and thereby led to his spiritual decay, taking him from bad to worse.

Although we see only these stages, perhaps the devil had prepared for these stages beforehand via several other steps of which we have no clue.

When the devil deals his final blow, he wants to ensure that it is deadly. This sometimes requires long preparations on his part so that when he comes, he may find the house adorned, furnished and ready for his work without any form of resistance. Or, even if his prey resists, he makes sure that they are made entirely powerless so that they may fall easily!

The story of Jacob the Struggler.

This story resembles the story of the fall of David as it gives a clear indication of how the devil carries out his plan of the 'long gradual attack'. Here the devil was able to lead a great hermit, who had the gift of exorcism, to fall into a grave sin. The devil was able to give this saint three deadly blows which would have destroyed him had not God's mercy led him to repentance.

The daughter of a certain king was possessed with an unclean spirit which no one could cast out. They brought her to St. Jacob the Struggler, who prayed for her and the unclean spirit was cast out but when she returned to her country, the spirit returned to her. They brought her again to the saint, he prayed for her and the spirit was cast out. Again as soon as she arrived in her country, the spirit returned once more and they brought her to the saint for the third time. **This trickery of the devil was repeated many times till they became weary of travelling repeatedly.**

At last, the king decided to leave the princess with the saint. They built a room for her nearby so that whenever the devil would return to her the saint could pray for her. Over time familiarity develop between them which ultimately led to sin – she conceived by Jacob. He feared the sin might be discovered and that the king would kill him as a result of it. The devil suggested that he kill her, so he killed her and buried her in a secluded place in the desert.

Months passed and the king's messengers came to inquire with regard to her safety. The saint concealed his second sin with a lie and told them that the devil had overthrown her once more, and that she had run out into the desert and escaped; they believed him due to his good reputation.

Thus, the devil gave him three blows by which he fell; adultery, murder and lying.

All this developed gradually over a long period of time - the beginning never suggested such an end. The devil, in his craftiness, weaves his traps with amazing patience.

The aim of this type of warfare is this: **that at every step the person becomes more familiar with sin, becomes used to it, and is thus made weaker.**

The individual's will may very well be strong while distant from sin, resenting every aspect of it. However, with nearness and time, they become accustomed to and familiar with it.

Gradually the idea of sin 'settles' in the mind and the heart. With every step the will weakens and becomes unable to resist, whether or not the person is aware of it.

An indication or result of these long, gradual wars are the bad habits we develop.

Any habit which dominates a person does not begin as such. It is possible the person has control over it at first and is able to stop performing this act or acting upon this habit. By the gradual and long-winded warfare by the devil the individual loses control over it. It dominates them.

The devil initially prods the person with the idea - *"Try"* or *"Test."* Then he advances with the lie that, *"All life is experience. You have control over the matter; you can abstain whenever you want."* He goes on pressing till the person yields completely and they ultimately stop resisting or even lose the desire to resist!

However, getting rid of habits is possible for anyone who wants to.

The devil may tell you that you are not able, or that even if you were able you will easily return to the habit again. It is a form of despair which fights you but do not yield. A habit results from a repeated willful act and you can counteract this through an 'opposite', repeated and willful act of fighting - be steady in such an act.

To resist the gradual war set forth by the devil, avoid the first step of his advance with all vigour and firmness no matter how innocent it may seem or how much the devil fights you to take it.

Beware of his lies, especially the lie of telling you that this initial advance is a single step which cannot lead to negative consequences.

10. 'Small' matters.

Heed the advice of the bride in the Song of Songs: *"Catch us the foxes, the little foxes that spoil the vines…"* (Song. 2:15).

We are warned; Though they are little, they spoil the vines.

The first danger of these small foxes (i.e. sins) is that they can more easily enter the soul. Big foxes do not easily find a hole wide enough for them in the hedge of the vineyard (of our souls) while the little ones can enter easily.

The devil may find one who is on guard against the great sins; one who easily avoids these sins. In this case, the devil postpones fighting them with these sins and begins using smaller matters, smaller sins, to fight the individual.

The devil fights with smaller matters as a person is less likely to guard against them, nor are they as anxious about

how it may affect them.

"Beware of offences" (Mat. 18:7); what does this mean?

If you say to someone for example, *"Beware of offences,"* he will reply in astonishment, *"Offences! Does one like me fear such tiny matters! They may fight those who are young or beginners but as for me, I have grown beyond such matters."* In like manner does the devil fight them.

Who would have thought that our father Abraham, the beloved of God, would become anxious and say in fear that his wife Sarah was his sister so that he would not be killed by one who would desire her!

Fear and deceit are among the tiny matters which the devil used against exceedingly great and spiritual men like our father Abraham, the father of all fathers – how much worse then are the tiny matters which are used against us!

It is not necessary that one commits a great sin such as adultery to be defiled but it is sufficient to commit a sin of the tongue that, *"...defiles the whole body..."* (James 3:6).

The tongue is a *"little member"* but it is *"...a world of iniquity"* and *"It is an unruly evil, full of deadly poison"* (James 3:8). It defiles the whole person, as the Lord has said, *"Not what goes into the mouth defiles a man; but what comes out of the mouth, this defiles a man..."* (Matt. 15:11). What is amazing is that the devil convinces you that the sins of the tongue are a small matter.

Indeed, the devil of tiny matters can destroy a person.

Consider how a ship is made to sink due to a small hole. It is not necessary that a person be devoured by a huge beast so that they may die but a tiny microbe, invisible to the naked eye, may perform this job sufficiently. The Lord said in the Sermon on the Mount;
"But I say to you that whoever is angry with his brother without a cause shall be in danger of the judgment..." (Matt. 5:22).

How easy it is for the devil to convince you that the word 'fool' and the like are among the small matters! Perhaps Ananias and Sapphira, who perished due to their deceit, thought that their sin was among the small matters. Perhaps Solomon thought that his multiple marriages to foreigners was a small thing, however it resulted in him almost losing his salvation (1 Kings 11:1 -11).

The 'tiny matters' are not in fact tiny at all.

The devil suggests them as 'tiny' and instills within us this name through his deceit. They very easily lead to dangerous results, such as what occurred in the cases of Solomon, David and Ananias.

God seeks to test our will with any test, however simple it seems, in order to reveal our inner state; as He did with Adam and Eve by setting before them the tree of the knowledge of good and evil.

What are examples of these 'tiny' matters?

A person who stubbornly holds his own opinions in high regard and is unwilling to change them or discuss them with anyone is an example of a person who has fallen into a 'small' matter. The devil may say to him, *"What of it? What is wrong with acting in this way? Is there any need to consult others? Is not your reasoning* sufficient?" However this can very well be the stepping stone by which the person learns to disregard the advice of their confession father. Other examples include becoming indulgent in satisfying the senses (which can lead to gluttony), becoming lax in controlling the material you hear and read, or losing the ability or desire to blame oneself for one's faults.

The way we are saved from the devil of tiny matters is through living a life of strictness.

Another way is through holding onto the virtue of being 'faithful in the little', for the Lord says, *"He who is faithful in what is least is faithful also in much..."* (Luke 16:10).

11. Postponement.

The devil tries by any and all means to prevent you from spiritual practices.

If he finds you insisting on performing spiritual practices, he calls on you to postpone.

He says to you, *"Why are you rushing? The matter is in our hands, we can perform it at any time. Perhaps taking our time gives us the chance to better examine the matter or to choose the easiest means to do it. Anyway, we have more important matters in hand which we must consider and perform first, before we begin to even consider this matter."*

The purpose of postponement is so that we lose the zeal we originally had to perform the task, so that we may lose the opportunity to do it or are forced to put the matter aside and do something which requires greater urgency.

For example, something which requires all your attention and time comes up or an event takes place which delays you, or certain obstacles arise which make it difficult to do what you sought to do in the first place. The devil may throw in your path a sin which causes you to lose your spiritual zeal so that you do not perform what you intended to and postpone it.

Remember the lost son, who acted immediately upon the desire to rise and go to his father (Luke 15:18-20). Had he postponed, who knows what his end would have been.

Among the examples of the harms of postponement are what happened to Felix the Governor and King Agrippa.

While St. Paul was speaking of righteousness, self control and the judgment to come, Felix trembled and told St. Paul, *"Go away for now; when I have a convenient time I will call for you."* (Acts 24:25). Due to his postponement, Felix lost the benefit of St. Paul's words and never called for St. Paul.

As for King Agrippa, when St. Paul was pleading before him, St. Paul said to him, *"King Agrippa, do you believe the prophets? I know that you believe."* (Acts 26:27) Then Agrippa said to Paul, *"You almost persuade me to become a Christian."* (Acts 26:28). By postponing, Agrippa did not benefit from the persuasiveness of St Paul's words, for we see no mention of his conversion.

Grace may only affect you once. If you postpone, its potential to impact your life may be lost.

You have the opportunity in hand - so do the work of God. Do not slacken or postpone because postponement may very well lead you to completely forget the task which is before you. This is the intention of the devil. He does not prevent you directly but he does so tactfully, via postponement – so beware of his wiles.

Do not postpone repentance, prayer or any good act you can perform.

It says in the Bible, *"Do not withhold good from those to whom it is due, when it is in the power of your hand to do so. Do not say to your neighbor; Go, and come back, And tomorrow I will give it; When you have it with you..."* (Prov. 3:27-28).

Although this concerns performing good towards others, this concerns the individual also. Whenever the Spirit of God speaks within you, do not postpone responding to His call, for the Apostle said more than once, *"Today, if you will hear His voice, do not harden your hearts..."* (Heb. 3:7-8).

Thus, postponement is a form of hardening your heart.

When the devil calls you to postpone, he is in fact calling you to be hard-hearted or to become accustomed to hard-heartedness, in order to ensure that you remain estranged from God.

12. Involvement (or business).

The devil wants to hinder you from any spiritual act you practice by making you get involved in many other things. He never wants to allow you the time in which you may sit with God or with yourself as he fears this would separate you from him and attach you to God.

When the devil finds that you are regular in your prayers and in reading, in attending spiritual meetings and in practices which increase God's love in your heart, he fights you by involving you temporarily or permanently in the work of the world.

This involvement may be taking on an additional job.

In this case, you find no time to devote yourself to God. The devil convinces you that such work is necessary for your livelihood and that you cannot be without it. He may also convince a person to undertake some form of higher studies or research to improve their academic level - they finish one form of study only to begin another.

This involvement may even be in the form of services in the church which take away time from your prayers. There is no objection to service but it must be within certain limits so as not to hinder prayer, contemplation or spiritual reading, all of which are ultimately used to increase your attachment to God.

This is necessary not only for the spiritual condition of the servant but for the success of the service as well.

When a servant becomes too greatly involved in various matters their spirit fails, resulting in the service losing its success and its positive influence upon those it affected. The lethargic spiritual life of the servant causes his service to become like a job, routine and rationalistic, no longer affecting the heart or soul of the people that serve or those they serve.

Many are the servants who are involved in so many various activities that they do not find time for a prayer or a psalm or any time to be alone with God. They live relying upon their past spiritual stock and are thus at risk of going to perdition.

The devil here does not fight the carrying out of spiritual practices but gives the person no time to perform them.

He does not prevent you from prayer, contemplation, and reading, nor from spiritual songs and hymns, kneeling down in worship or examining yourself. He may even allow you to give lessons and lectures on such spiritual practices and their benefit - but gives you no time to practice them yourself. Thus you become, as one of the spiritual fathers said, like bells which call people to the sanctuary but do not enter themselves! How truly powerful are the words of one of the spiritual fathers, *"You spent your whole life serving the Lord's house, when will you serve the Lord of the house?"*

If this is the condition of servants, how about ordinary people with their many responsibilities?

There are visits to friends houses, gossip, arguments and discussions, newspapers, magazines, the news and the commentaries on them, and the abundant means of entertainment which are available both to the old and the young. Consider, for example, football, and how much time people spend on following it, becoming invested in the emotions of the sport, the enthusiasm and the commentaries! There are also their intellectual and social involvements, their problems and cares, and the financial and economic affairs of the country and world around them.

Even children are involved in television programs, tales and games which stop them from going to church. The grown-ups are also attracted to their programs and are hindered by them!

God looks from His heavens upon the world and finds it to be a busy one.

It is a world which runs quickly and does not take the time to think about where it is going! It is a clamorous world filled with constant talking, noise, discussion and agitation. Where then is the quietude necessary for the spiritual life? You seek it and often do not find it!

Even many of the clergymen who have devoted themselves to the Lord and who should be '*His portion*' are busy; separated from God by many things! The war which fought Martha still exists and continues to be made evident in our present world; *"You are worried and troubled about many things; but one thing is needed..."* (Luke 10:42). As for you who are God's children and image, you must develop and have a spiritual character.

Let God be the one who directs and is sovereign over your life and your commitments.

Let your spiritual practices, your attachment to God and your life with God be your priority; prioritising your time so that everything related to the church and getting closer to God comes first. Give priority to your salvation and your eternity - only then arrange your other responsibilities (no matter how urgent they may seem). Remember the words of the Lord;

"For what profit is it to a man if he gains the whole world, and loses his own soul?" (Matt. 16:26).

If you lose your own soul, what shall you give in exchange for it? All those who died and departed from the world, what did all their involvements avail them? And when they left those matters upon their death, did the world suffer confusion? Of course not, as the wise Solomon said of this world;

"All was vanity and grasping for the wind. There was no profit under the sun..." (Eccl. 2:11)

Start your day with God before any other involvement. Let God be, *'In the beginning'* and say to Him, *"O God, You are my God; Early will I seek You; My soul thirsts for You..."* (Ps. 63:1). Arrange your time so that no other involvement prevails over the time which you spend with God. Do not go out of your house before you perform all your spiritual duties and do not give priority to anything over your spiritual matters, whatever its profit, its value or its importance may be.

The devil always exaggerates the importance of the things that hinder us.

He tempts us exceedingly with such matters. In fact, nothing at all in your life is more important than God. You ought not to sacrifice your relationship with God for anything or any person, no matter who they are.

The Lord Himself says, *"He who loves father or mother... son or daughter more than Me is not worthy of Me."* (Matt. 10:37). How much more then is this true for worldly matters!

So, if any new involvement comes to you, consider wisely before accepting it.

The devil may not be satisfied by the hindrance your current involvements present and thus may be placing other responsibilities upon you which you cannot bear. Every day he will suggest to you things which may appear to provide you with great benefit, however you must be on guard against these suggestions. Learn to put your spirituality ahead of anything else, no matter how useful it may appear to be.

Worldly involvements are a wile of the devil to lead you astray from God. However there is another wile which is all the more cunning, namely:

13. Misunderstanding God's love.

No one doubts God's love for us and the importance of our love for Him but the devil may instill within us an idea of God's love which is misleading. He convinces people that they can sin as they please, knowing that God's love 'protects us'; depending (without true conviction and in the wrong manner) upon God's love, mercy and forgiveness and the salvation granted us upon the cross!

It is as if they think God's love allows us to be reckless and lazy in following His commandments. God forbid that any should think this! The Holy Bible states, *"...do you despise the riches of His goodness, forbearance, and longsuffering, not knowing that the goodness of God leads you to repentance. But in accordance with your hardness and your impenitent heart you are treasuring up for yourself wrath in the day of wrath..."* (Rom. 2:4,5); and further, *"Therefore consider the goodness and severity of God: on those who fell, severity; but toward you, goodness, if you continue in His goodness. Otherwise you also will be cut off,"* (Rom. 11:22).

The devil presents God's love in a way so as to make one lose the fear of God!

He distorts, to a great extent, the words of St. John, *"There is no fear in love; but perfect love casts out fear."* (1 John 4:18). In this manner, he tries to remove God's fear from the hearts of people using the name of love, contradicting the words of the Bible: *"The fear of the LORD is the beginning of wisdom."* (Ps. 111:10).

There is a book that I wanted to publish about 'The fear of God' and the relationship between this form of fear and love.

I prepared the material for this book more than a year ago and announced that I would release it – however, I postponed publishing it. Now I feel that it is necessary to publish this book, as it has become fashionable for people to use God's love as an excuse to do away with spiritual caution and watchfulness. All of this is due to the intrigues of the devil!

Indeed, God is very loving and willing to forgive our iniquities but He is also just in His actions and Holy in His character.

Just as God has no limits to His love, He too has no limits to His justice and holiness. His holiness does not accept sin, and His justice punishes it.

We have so far only mentioned how we misunderstand God's love for us; how about our love for God?

The devil tricks us into loving God merely with our emotions!

Our love for God should in fact be a practical love; *"Let us not love in word or in tongue, but in deed and in truth…"* (1 John 3:18). Whoever loves God does not disobey Him nor provokes Him to anger. Our love for God depends on our obedience to Him and keeping His commandments. As the Lord has said, *"If you keep My commandments, you will abide in My love."* (John 15:10); and, *"If anyone loves Me, he will keep My word…"* (John 14:23). St. John the beloved also said, *"For this is the love of God, that we keep His commandments."* (1 John 5:3). To love God means that we do not love the world and all its lusts, for the Bible states, *"If anyone loves the world, the love of the Father is not in him…"* (1 John 2:15) and *"…friendship with the world is enmity with God."* (Jam. 4:4).

Let not the devil deceive you and say to you, *"It is enough to love God and do whatever you want!"*

14. Corrupting principles and values.

The devil wages a mental war upon the world; one in which he seeks to plant and develop new principles and concepts that secretly serve his purpose.

In this war, he tries to destroy our values, traditions and all established ideas.

He throws people into doubt concerning them and accuses whoever holds to old traditions of being obscure, backwards, old-fashioned and uncivilised! It is as if old traditions are an insult to modern society and must be destroyed!

It is a revolution of the devil against Christian (and even basic civil) values and beliefs.

The devil wants a trend of sin – that all may fall into practicing, as if it were normal and acceptable. He wants that anyone who is not part of this trend to be attacked and mocked by society! This has led to things that we might call intuitive or normal to be called into question and to become matters of discussion. What is virtue? What is religion? What are our rights and duties? What are our family values?

The devil has bred within this generation a concept or idea of liberty which is blatantly wrong.

Through this concept the devil seeks to convince man that he is free to do what he wants, to adopt whatever ideas or beliefs he likes and to spread them without restriction, no matter how wrong such ideas, beliefs or behaviours might be and despite the negative consequences these things may have.

We currently have a system in which we do not accept, rightly so, the concept of absolute freedom. A person is able to exercise their freedom so long as they do not invade another's rights and liberties and so long as they uphold the values and morals of the society around them. If one was able to exercise their freedom without constraint, we would find ourselves in a world of anarchy, without morals or ethics!

God has given man liberty but He has given with it certain commandments which must be followed. God will judge how man uses this liberty and will punish him if he causes any harm to himself or others in using it.

The devil calls for an absolute freedom which is highly dangerous - a freedom which allows for dangerous beliefs and behaviours to develop.

An example with regard to behaviour is the kind of liberty that 'hippies', atheist, existentialists etc. seek to exercise. They find no shame in walking naked in the streets or in partaking of sexual acts unashamedly, performing that which disgraces common human decency. Further examples consist of the nihilistic ideology (and other such ideologies) that have caused society to both question what is in fact the 'correct way' of thinking and adopt ideas which will and have caused our corruption. The devil encourages all this in the name of the deceptive idea he has created of liberty, disregarding the liberty which God has planned for us.

True liberty is that a person becomes free from their faults and sinful passions – that they become free from their lusts and sinful desires; from the habits which dominate them and have caused them to lose their free will without their notice.

If one were to recognise those desires within them that are

corrupt and yet chose to remain subject to them - to remain subject to the flesh and that which is material - what then would be the result?

Surely, a world dominated by its desires will hate God, for He resists such desires. Thus, the devil has achieved his ultimate aim!

The devil desires to make people hate God and wants that they consider Him their enemy.

He achieves this under the pretense that God takes away their liberty, that He makes their existence worthless and stands in the way of their desires! Then, instead of correcting such desires and seeking purity, these people hold fast to their sinfulness and become enemies of God because of it!

The devil also seeks to spread and achieves in spreading unrestricted liberty with respect to theological understanding.

He causes everyone to interpret the Bible as they like, understand what they want and spread their own understanding. Thus, the minds of people become confused and muddled in the face of hundreds - if not thousands - of different interpretations. Hundreds of sects have appeared in Christianity due to this corrupt understanding of liberty, by which people come to believe everyone is free to have their beliefs and do not need to submit to any form of religious authority!

The church has one faith; it is not a collection of several contradicting beliefs.

The Holy Bible teaches one faith, for it states, *"One Lord, one faith, one baptism..."* (Eph. 4:5) - also; *"Now the multitude of those who believed were of one heart and one soul..."* (Acts 4:32). The Holy Bible teaches that the church is one body, with Christ as the head, no matter how abundant its members may be (Eph. 5:23). Since its head is Christ, it must always have the mind of Christ (1 Cor. 2:16) – a singular mind that leaves no room for contradictions to exist.

What then about freedom of belief and its limits?

We do not object to everyone having the freedom to believe whatever they want.

It is impossible to make someone believe in something in spite of their will but whoever holds to the beliefs of the church becomes a member of it and whoever refuses its beliefs remains outside of it, for the church maintains its single and united faith.

The church does not invade the liberty of any person or force them to believe but:

Nobody may claim to be a member of a church in whose principles and beliefs they do not believe.

Here the devil cannot argue a case for liberty because though it exists, no one may be accepted as a member of a church except one who holds to its beliefs. It is a self-evident truth. So, if a person does not hold to the beliefs of the church, they have abandoned it by their free will. The words of St. John the beloved apply to them; *"They went out from us, but they were not of us; for if they had been of us, they would have continued with us."* (1 John 2:19).

We mention this here because in the name of 'freedom of belief', lectures in theological colleges around the world teach whatever they want without adhering to the creed of the church to which they belong or whose beliefs they teach. A professor comes to the lecture and teaches whatever he likes!

It has also given atheist professors the chance to teach theology in some colleges!

Hence, under the name of freedom and liberty, the devil has been able to accomplish his plan successfully!

As for the apostolic universal church which holds to, *"The faith which was once for all delivered to the saints..."* (Jude 1:3), it has never permitted this. It condemned heretics and those who sought to deceive the church and excommunicated them in order to keep the one faith of the church so that it may soundly be taught to the coming generations. St. Paul the Apostle says authoritatively, *"But even if we, or an angel from heaven, preach any other gospel to you than what we have preached to you, let him be accursed."* (Gal. 1:8). St. John the beloved says, *"If anyone comes to you and does not bring this doctrine, do not receive him into your house nor greet him: For he who greets him shares in his evil deeds..."* (2 John 1:10-11) - this coming from the Apostle who spoke of love more than any other Apostle.

The church has always guarded the faith and defended it from any potential deviation or heresy as a result of private interpretation or ideas; things which people now accept in the name of 'liberty'.

For this reason, we find that the devil despises any form of church authority and fights clerical authority.

We find the following to be a rule in our faith; whoever deviates from the orthodox faith and is unrepentant will definitely begin fighting against clerical authority as if they have the God-given power to condemn any heretical ideas (Matt. 18:18, John 20:23).

The devil seeks to spread his thoughts and ideas in every area of human existence, not only as a means of fighting the church. He uses a well-known device to do so: **Resistance to authority**.

He means, of course, to resist any form of authority that will not accept any deviation or incorrect teaching to enter. He fights them, seeking to undermine their authority and/or prevent their work. His purpose is to make that which is wrong become the accepted and 'right' behavior.

He fights:

- the authority of the father in the family in order the defend the ability of the son to 'express his personality'.
- the authority of the teacher in school or college under the pretext of empowering the next generation.
- the authority of the state in the name of democracy and defending people's rights.
- God's right to have the ultimate authority of man!
- the clergy's authority as stewards of God, responsible for His flock (Tit. 1:7).

The devil desires that there may be no 'watchman' who may see through his deception; no one who finds the faults he spreads and corrects them.

He does this seeking to contradict the words of God, *"I have made you a watchman... therefore hear a word from My mouth and give them warning from Me."* (Ezek. 3:17). The devil desires all matters to remain without someone in control or watching over them. He desires 'rash freedom', as was seen in the book of Judges; *"In those days there was no king in Israel; everyone did what was right in his own eyes."* (Judg. 17:6).

15. Following the general trend.

The general trend may be sinful and the devil calls you to submit to such a trend and become a part of it. He may whisper in your ears, **"Everyone is like this. Why should you be an exception to the rule and have your own way?"**

You must respond saying, *"We follow the truth no matter if the majority believe it or not. If the majority is wrong, we do not follow it, just as our father Noah; for all the people in his time were wicked but he and his family alone were righteous."*

It is not unlikely that the majority or a whole generation may be wrong.

At the time of the cross, the majority were wrong and cried out, *"Crucify Him, crucify Him!"* (Luke 23:21) and Christ Himself said of the whole generation that it was; *"An evil and adulterous generation,..."* (Matt. 12:39).

During the reign of King Ahab, the majority worshipped idols except for seven thousand from among hundreds of thousands (1 Kin. 19:18). At the time of Moses the prophet, the Lord condemned the people for their rebellious and stiff-necked nature and did not allow any of them to enter the promised land except Joshua the son of Nun and Caleb the son of Jephunneh (Num. 14:20-30). The man of God who is firm in following His commandments and living by the truth can sing;

***"I shall obey God and Him alone I shall obey."* However, the devil forces people to follow the general trend by every means necessary.**

Sometimes, he causes people to follow that which is the wrong out of 'courtesy', or due to an individual's shyness or by intimidation or for fear of people's mockery or reproach or due to pressures from others or in response to the devil who says, *"You will only get this opportunity once!"* Another person may keep up with the current social trend in submission to an authority more powerful than themselves, or to a superior, or out of ignorance. The devil may say to them;

"Is it possible that all people are wrong and you alone are right?"

"Is it possible that the majority does not know what is good and right and you alone know? Humble yourself, for what do you know?" The person is convinced and follows the trend.

He may also follow the trend due to the influence of a sinful friend or companion who attracts them to their way, just as Solomon followed after the ways of the women he married (1 Kin. 11:4).

A person may also submit to the social trends as a result of their weak personality.

They cannot resist, or resist a little, and then are unable to continue. It is amazing how the people of this world are powerful in defending their wrong doings and in mocking God's children who do not follow their way. They mock them in order that their resolve may be weakened and that they may be caused to submit. What a pity!

God's children must be strong in following their principles, remaining firm, steady, and unmovable against the mockery of the wicked. They have to remember the words of the Bible, *"...have no fellowship with the unfruitful works of darkness, but rather expose them..."* (Eph. 5:11).

If they cannot reprove the works of darkness, they must at least not be a part of them. They must have a distinctive way of life; one which follows the words of St. John the beloved, *"In this the children of God and the children of the devil are manifest,"* (1 John 3:10). It is also said, *"You will know them by their fruits."* (Matt. 7:16) and *"...your speech betrays you..."* (Matt. 26:73). St. Paul the Apostle affirms further, *"...do not be conformed to this world..."* (Rom. 12:2).

Do not put on its form, nor be like those who are in it. Your form and your origin is known; you are made in the image and likeness of God as God Himself said; *"Let Us make man in Our image, according to Our likeness."* (Gen. 1:26). How can you give up your divine image and make yourself in the image of this corrupt and fallen world?

Daniel and the three saintly youth had 'power' over the general trend.

From the beginning of their coming to the king's palace, they refused the king's food and did not eat with the others who were with them. How beautiful are the words of the Bible; *"...Daniel purposed in his heart that he would not defile himself with the portion of the king's delicacies, nor with the wine which he drank."* (Dan. 1:8). Daniel and the three young men insisted on following the commandments of God, though they were captives of war, under the authority of others and serving as slaves in the king's palace. In their hearts and souls they were free and unrestricted, not submitting to the general trend but to God's will.

Following their example, be brave, be firm in your principles and resist what it is that those around you accept as normal if it is wrong. Do not submit to the devil, his advice and the fears which he seeks to arouse within you. Refuse anything wrong even if you find those who are older doing it. If you find those who follow the right way are very few do not be disheartened, for those who are selected are few. As the Lord has said, *"...narrow is the gate and difficult is the way, which leads to life, and there are few who find it."* (Matt. 7:14). Know that, though the majority falls in committing that which is wrong, this does not make what is wrong right.

The wrong is wrong and the falling of the majority in such wrong does not justify it. It is known that the right way is difficult and that not all people can follow it; only the few distinguished for their principles and their integrity can truly follow it. If you find that the devil has instilled fear within all, do not fear. If you find that the majority has fallen into insincerity and flattery, do not do the same thing. If you find that all have followed the worldly means of amusement, entertainment, luxury and fashion, do not do the same thing. If you find that the language of the people has changed and differed from before, insist on sticking to what you know to be right.

If your resistance against the current is weakened, say with the psalmist;

"You shall keep them, O LORD, You shall preserve them from this generation forever." (Ps. 12:7).

The Lord is able to save you from the current of this world and from its potential to sweep you away.

16. Temptations.

Since the first sin, the devil has been offering temptations to his victims in order to make them fall. The first temptation he offered to our forefathers was, *"You will be like God, knowing good and evil..."* (Gen 3:5). He went on tempting men with, *"...the lust of the flesh, the lust of the eyes, and the pride of life."* (1 John 2:16). An example of one who was greatly tempted despite his virtue was King Solomon (Eccl. 2:1-10).

On the mount, the devil offered the Lord Jesus Christ three temptations; turning stone into bread, sending angels to bear Him up in their hands and giving Him all the kingdoms and glory of the world (Matt. 4). The Lord refused all these, disgracing the devil and causing him to flee.

The temptations of the devil entrap only the heart that is

inclined to accept them.

But a strong heart refuses such temptations i.e. is not tempted by them. Queen Jezebel sought to influence King Jehu and lure him into her control as King Ahab had been before him, so, *"...she put paint on her eyes and adorned her head..."* (2 Kin. 9:30). But Jehu was not tempted by this false beauty; he disdained it and ordered that she be killed.

The devil sometimes plans his temptations and in other cases tests the 'pulse' of the individual to see what temptations will work.

He feels the pulse to see whether his victim becomes weak before certain temptations or not. If he finds that the person does not care for it or is not affected by it, he attempts another temptation as he did with the Lord Jesus Christ, whom he found strong before all the temptations he set before Him. Due to the vast experience of the devil, he chooses for each person what temptation he thinks fits them.

He may tempt the person with something that he knows him to be in need of.

He tempted the Lord Jesus Christ with bread when, *"...He was hungry..."* (Matt. 4:2). He tempted King Saul with divination when he was in need of counsel and did not find it (1 Sam. 28: 4-7).

He tempted the Israelites with the molten calf at the time in which he found fit - while Moses the prophet was away from the people and the Israelites were left with no spiritual guidance (Ex. 32:1-4).

The temptation offered by the devil is strong and effective. It is used to hinder repentance and any spiritual acts.

If he finds a person insisting on repentance with all their might, he offers them a sin for which they have longed for and have been seeking without success. He puts it suddenly before them in order that they do not have time to react and are made to fall. If someone has stopped reading certain offensive books, the devil will send them on that day a friend offering them one of these books which the victim longed to buy for many months but has not been able to find. They find themselves weak before the temptation - they read and fall. If a youth repents from adultery, they find that the sin seeks them of its own accord.

The poor person thinks it is an 'irrecoverable chance' and the devil says to him, *"Do not miss the opportunity. You can repent afterwards! "*

Thus, whenever the devil finds someone seeking to move away from sin, he offers him the greatest temptations; those temptations which reopen the most painful and sensitive wounds of the soul. So, if you repent and find that a sin seeks you with great perseverance **do not say,** *"It is an opportunity"* **but say,** *"Certainly it is the work of the devil."*

It is not something natural or something that happens by coincidence but it is a well-designed plan of the devil. Blessed is the Lord who reveals it to us in order that we might escape it. As the holy monk, father Abdel Messeih El-Habashi (the Ethiopian), the solitary anchorite in the Shiheet desert, says, *"A trap, father, a trap..."*

17. 'Drugging'.

When a person is wakeful and aware of his own salvation, attentive in mind and soul, it is difficult for him to fall. Thus, one of the saints said, *"A sin is preceded either by lust, unawareness or forgetfulness; the last two are used as a means by which the devil drugs a person."*

Being drugged in this way, a person is driven into sin as if he were unconscious of what was happening!

Thus, it is well said of the repentance of the lost son that, *"...he came to himself..."* (Luke 15:17). The word 'came' indicates that he was not conscious or at least not completely conscious during the time he spent in sin. So when he came to himself he began to think in a way which was different to how he did while he was in his sin.

The devil drugs the person so as to make them forget everything except sin.

All their senses, thoughts and emotions become concentrated on the sin alone. They become totally unaware of anything else, as if they have forgotten completely how to live without it.

They forget that they are made in the image of God. They forget His commandments and the results of following them. They forget their spiritual level, practices, canon and cautiousness. They forget God's promises and their own undertakings and vows. They forget to keep their guard up and may even forget that they may be fasting or those days which are meant to be holy and consecrated to the Lord. They forget the punishment and warnings of God as if they were completely drugged. The devil has drugged them with the sin and they have become unaware of anything else.

They come to themselves only after falling, when everything has reached its conclusion.

David the prophet was drugged when he fell and was driven from one sin to another. He did not regain consciousness until he heard Nathan the prophet address him with the words, *"You are the man."* (2 Sam. 12:7). Only then did he come to himself and truly feel the extent of his sin!

Cain was also 'drugged' when he arose and killed his brother. He came to himself only upon hearing the words from the Lord, *"Where is Abel your brother?"* (Gen. 4:9). Only then did he come to himself and feel the impact of his detestable deed and its result, exclaiming, *"My punishment is greater than I can bear!"* (Gen. 4:13).

A person may come to themselves immediately after their fall or only after an extended length of time.

The prodigal son did not come to himself except after he had spent all his money and was in want, finally realising the miserable state he found himself in (Luke 15:14-17). The rich man, the contemporary of the poor Lazarus, did not come to himself except when he found himself in hell (Luke 16:19-23).

St. Peter came to himself almost immediately, weeping bitterly after denying the Lord (Matt. 26:75), while Judas did not come to himself except when the chance to do so had disappeared.

There are some who come to themselves and repent, while others come to themselves and become despondent and depressed.

The prodigal son, David the Prophet and St. Peter the Apostle came to themselves and repented but Judas, when he came to himself, was led by the devil to despair and, *"...he went and hanged himself."* (Matt. 27:3-5). He died in his sin and perished.

Thus, I give you two pieces of advice which you ought to follow when the devil 'drugs' you.

The first piece of advice is to come to yourself quickly. In the words of the Psalmist, *"... awaken the dawn..."* (Ps. 57:8) and be wary that you do not remain drugged by sin for such a length of time that it becomes a habit. Otherwise it will be difficult for you to recover your consciousness and you will find - after coming to yourself - that you have reached a terrible state.

The second piece of advice is that, when you come to yourself, let your repentance be sincere and occur without delay; do not repent in despair but do so in hope and in joy, knowing that God forgives sinners. Use repentance and penitence in your spiritual life in order to gain true benefit.

18. Turning religion into philosophy.

The Lord Jesus Christ desired that religion be spirit and life (John 6:63).

Thus He said, *"The words that I speak to you are spirit, and they are life."* (John 6:63). That means that we should understand the spirit of the Word and turn it into life within us.

Religion becomes a means for purification of the heart and the means by which we learn to cleave to God, with the ultimate aim of attaining eternal life with Him. Perhaps this is what the Lord meant by the words, *"I have come that they may have life, and that they may have it more abundantly."* (John 10:10).

But the devil desires to turn religion solely into a platform for arguments and discussion.

He desires that reasoning replaces spirit and arguments replace practice – thus, the religious life becomes one of reasoning; Christianity becomes treated as a philosophy which is studied and analysed. Christianity becomes a subject to be taught and not a life to lead. The devil revels in this, for his plans are not affected by one who learns about Christianity rather than lives it – this is what the devil wants.

There is a book by St. Augustine entitled "Contra Academicos" which is translated to, "Against the Academics." I wish I could translate for you some of the paragraphs contained within it, for St. Augustine fights specifically this problem of viewing Christianity as a philosophy.

The reasoning system which the devil desires to plant within Christian believers is fought by St. Paul the Apostle.

In the first two chapters of St. Paul's First Epistle to the Corinthians he says; *"When I came to you, I did not come with excellence of speech or of wisdom,..."* and *"...my speech and my preaching were not with persuasive words of human wisdom, but in demonstration of the Spirit and of power."* (1 Cor. 2:1, 4).

Further he states; *"For Christ did not send me to baptize, but to preach the gospel, not with wisdom of words, lest the cross of Christ should be made of no effect..."* (1 Cor. 1:17). How dangerous it is then to focus on the academics of Christianity if it causes the Cross of Christ to be of no effect!

Heresies arose as a mental attack of the devil in order to hinder the spiritual growth of those within the church.

During the era of martyrdom in the first three centuries and at the beginning of the fourth century and during the development and propagation of monastic life at the end of the third century (which flourished in the fourth and fifth centuries), the church saw its members gain a growing love for God under the guidance of mighty spiritual fathers such as St. Anthony, St. Athanasius and the like. This aroused the envy of the devil and thus he sought some means by which he may halt this progress – by getting people caught up in arguments and discussions of theology for two long centuries (the fourth and the fifth). Hence arose the heresies of Arius, Apollinarius, Sabilius, Macedonius, Nestorius, Eutychus and others. All this took place in quick succession, puzzling the minds of Christians around the world. Discussion with regard to the divinity and nature of the Son went on in the streets, even amongst the common people. The devil offered to these heretics concepts and interpretations of verses of the Bible which were not founded on the teachings of the Apostles. Fathers of the church found themselves involved in refuting these heresies and heterodoxies for a long period of time.

The devil desires that our whole lives be filled with mental debates and refutations in order for us to be too 'busy' to truly follow God.

It is his scheme that in every generation he sends someone who attempts to turn religion into discussion, arguments, reasoning, debates, views and refutations. Wishing by this to hinder true spirituality on the one hand and to propagate controversy and division on the other; the devil rejoices when he sees the church divided into different parties and sects. Those who fall into heresy do it to the devils' benefit and those who are offended and confused are to his benefit also and those who stop their spiritual struggle because of vain arguments and controversy that arise do so to his gain also.

Let us thank God that the fathers who refuted the heresies that arose were deeply spiritual men.

Take for example St. Athanasius and his book "On the Incarnation." You will find this to be a book which is both edifying to the spirit as well as a source of sound theology and a teaching of the fundamental creeds of a Christian; in contrast to others who did, or still do, spend their time simply debating for the sake of it. It is also through the guidance of God that the period in which these heretical ideas arose (during the fourth and fifth centuries) occurred side by side with the growth of the monastic movement and the spiritual guidance that it provided so that there was some sort of 'balance' which allowed the church to keep true to its original teachings.

Refutation of heresies was necessary in order to ensure that we kept the original orthodox faith but for everyone to be busy doing so was a hindrance to the church. However, God did not leave His people and ultimately made this period in the church a positive one by establishing a firmer faith in the hearts of the believers, removing any doubts they may have had.

The devil even tries to turn spiritual matters into philosophy.

For example, he may turn prayer into an ideology made up of certain rules rather than the deepening of a relationship with God. He does the same thing with monastics; he sets different monasteries into conflict with regard to the best way for the community or monks to live; in solitude or as a community which works together, in isolated contemplation or in service of others. This discussion becomes a point of conflict which greatly pleases the devil.

Even the Lord's Prayer (Our Father) is turned by the devil into a conflict concerning translation (in the Arabic language specifically).

You find some people will say, *"Give us this day our daily bread..."* while others say, *"Give us this day our bread for the coming day."* Thus, there arises a conflict of translation and we find that instead of contemplating on the prayer itself, there arises an argument and discussion concerning the most accurate translation!

The same thing occurs in the Holy Liturgy. The different translations are an excuse the devil uses to wage a 'war of translation' in which he causes the members of the church to focus on fixing this 'problem' rather than focusing on what is truly important – the liturgy itself.

How easily he causes new thoughts to arise within the church itself.

He finds one who holds themselves in high esteem and believes they can pioneer a new change or development in the church and offers them a new interpretation or belief which diverges from what is accepted by the church. He tells this person that all who preceded him were wrong and did not see the truth as he does. Thus, instead of using their mental capacity to spread thoughts regarding religion which are filled with love and purity of heart, the devil corrupts their faculties and uses them to spread conflict and confusion among the people.

Taken to an extreme, this results in the formation of different parties, each claiming that they are defending the true faith and that their beliefs are true. The devil is then able to hinder the work of spiritual people by involving them in this culture of negativism and conflict. If they do not do so, the devil is able to freely spread doubt and confusion.

19. A period without sin.

The devil might stop fighting for a time if he finds that his warfare is not having the desired effect.

He stops fighting for a time, not out of his compassion for the person he is fighting but to lead them into a false sense of security which causes them to slacken and lose their initial caution. Then he returns to them with an even more severe war in order to overthrow them. In this way, he causes the person to lose trust in their ability to lead a life of righteousness and convinces them that though they may repent, they will certainly return to sin again. Or he takes the sin away from them for a period of time so that they may begin to long for it!

Perhaps the repeated practice of a sin may cause them to become bored with it and learn to hate it. So the devil takes it away from them for some time and then returns, fighting them with the sin in a more violent or desirable manner than before in order to cause them to fall more easily.

Thus, the devil 'grants' and 'prevents' sin in such a way so as to never give the person stability and to overcome them in the end.

He plays with the emotions and desires of the human soul. He causes it to be unstable, rising and falling. Those who are God's children become more cautious, careful and humble in these circumstances. However, the devil desires that they be in a constant state of fear and distrust, feeling that righteousness is beyond their ability. Thus, he moves gradually from this form of mental attack to a different type of attack in which he says, *"Christianity is a religion of sublimity and perfection but it is an impractical sublimity beyond the ability of one to attain."* At the same time, he hides from the person examples of the righteous people we find in every age.

20. The manifest bodily virtues.

He entices the person to have and practice the manifest (unhidden) bodily virtues rather than the hidden spiritual virtues.

The word 'manifest' here refers to those virtues which are apparent to the person themselves, not necessarily to others. By such virtues, the devil wants to cause them to fall into self-admiration and vanity, or disdain of others who have not attained the 'same level'.

This war is directed both at monks as well as laypeople.

When a monk begins his struggle in the monastic life, the devil causes them to be concerned with fasting, metanoias, watchfulness, silence and solitude, which are all visible acts. This is done in the hope of causing him to neglect the virtues of the heart such as love, joy, peace, purity, meekness and calmness.

During periods of fasting, the devil fights on the level of the body rather than the spirit.

He makes a person's whole concern the period and time of abstinence, the kind of food to be eaten, the necessity to abstain from foods that may be too decadent, decreasing the quantity of water one drinks - these are all matters concerning the body. He causes them to completely neglect the spiritual virtues related to fasting such as penitence, elevation of the spirit and self-control.

The devil knows that such fasting of the body alone does not in fact have any lasting benefit for the person spiritually. However, he deceptively uses this point afterwards in order to prevent the person from fasting, saying, *"Why fast when you have gained no benefit from it?"*

The same phenomenon takes place when it comes to kneeling down in worship (metanoias).

What concerns the devil is making the person increase the

number of metanoias they do continuously without understanding their benefit. He never allows the person to think that when they kneel down, their soul should cleave to the dust (Ps. 119:25) in humility and in recognition of their weaknesses. He causes them to neglect the spiritual aspect and the prayer that should accompany this action of the flesh; he wants that these metanoias, in spite of their abundance, become a bodily practice which will exert the individual but give them no benefit. This very easily leads them to vainglory!

As for seclusion, he cares only for its outward appearance and not the spirituality that should accompany it.

He desires that the person who lives in seclusion, for example, to live in it as if it were simply a change of location and outlook rather than a spiritual life characterised by certain virtues where the mind chooses to be alone with God in love and the heart remains completely dead to the world. The devil often causes the secluded hermit to become satisfied with simply residing in a cave away from the monastery. He fills the hermit's heart with pride and wrath against the monastery and its inhabitants, neglecting his spiritual practices inside the cave. True are the words of St. Isaac the Syrian. *"There may be a person who resides in a cell for 50 years not knowing how to occupy their time in their cell."*

What is said about seclusion also applies to silence.

The aim of silence is to prevent a person from committing the faults of the tongue, giving them a chance to talk to God. Yet, if a person is satisfied with silence alone, it becomes a 'manifest' act of the body, as they may still fall easily within their mind into all the faults they would have done with their tongue, such as condemning or reviling others, becoming angry and being sharp with their words. If the heart is at the same time not in communication with God, the silence will have no spiritual benefit.

In the same way, a person may be satisfied simply with living in physical virginity.

A person may think that virginity is the act of remaining unmarried, while the soul may not be chaste and the thoughts defiled. The positive or spiritual aspect of virginity is in directing all your love to God rather than a partner. If this does not exist, the person has the outer appearance of virginity but they do not have its spirit and have not achieved its effectiveness in the heart.

Our main concern should be directed towards the inner spiritual act, for this is what is most important.

For the Lord has said, *"My son, give me your heart..."* (Prov. 23:26). So, a person should begin first with purity of heart, attaining the true love of God and gaining the inner virtues.

From the pure heart comes forth strong and fervent prayer, prayerful metanoias, true and spiritual fasting and every other virtue. It is surprising how often that the person who cares for apparent bodily virtues disagrees with their father confessor, thinking themselves wiser than their confession father - and thinks of seeking another - while their interior life is not yet pure before God!

21. Violence.

This is a war which the devil directs both at the spiritual person and the beginner in the spiritual path, as well as the sinner.

The devil trains a person to be violent in combatting every source of wrong. Consequently, the person becomes violent towards everyone who contradicts their views. Behind such violence hides pride and hardheartedness.

We see that many people of the world (those who are spiritual) are distinguished for their meekness and calmness, while we find among those who call themselves followers of God some who are violent in the name of religion - dissatisfied with everything they see around them. They think that they alone know God and follow His ways. Through this violence, the devil causes them to fall into many faults which many laymen escape. He makes them forget virtues such as meekness and gentleness, which are the fruits of the Holy Spirit (Gal. 5:22).

22. Hindrances.

Every spiritual act is subject to many hindrances by the devil.

A person may set his heart on a certain spiritual act but the devil resists them with all his power in order to detain them from performing what they desired to do. As the Apostle says, *"For to will is present with me, but how to perform what is good I do not find."* (Rom. 7:18). These hindrances may be outer circumstances, forgetfulness, lack of time, resistance by the enemy or enemies, or false brethren. The devil then says;

"Decidedly, this act is not of God or He would have facilitated the means to perform it!"

Or he may say about a good person, *"Had this person truly been of God, God would have made him successful."* In this manner, the devil gives the person a bad reputation and causes people to stumble; he kills two birds with one stone.

23. Weakness in character.

Meekness is a virtue that is well-utilised by a person. However, the devil uses it in a way so as to further his aim of separating people from God.

For example, a person may be sitting among a group of people who begin uttering filthy words, defaming someone of rank, or telling inappropriate tales. The person, who does not welcome this sort of behavior thinks of withdrawing and leaving the group but the devil of bashfulness intercepts this thought and forces this person to stay. They stay and their mind becomes filled with thoughts which they would have avoided otherwise.

Also, as a result of shyness, they may sign a petition or agree to a nomination which their conscience does not agree with.

The person may sign a statement or decision which they are not content with in their heart or they may join in praising a person who does not deserve it. Even if they try to abstain, bashfulness prevents them!

The devil may also cause a young girl to become shy of dressing modestly.

This occurs if the general trend contradicts this kind of behaviour. The devil may also make her shy of being religious in general; shy of praying or fasting or of being known as someone who does so. She may even become shy of wearing a cross or refusing an invitation to a certain party which may be very harmful to her spiritual condition.

Likewise, a religious youth may find themselves too shy to refuse a cigarette offered them by a friend or a relative. How abundant are the sins in which some fall into due to the devil of bashfulness!

A religious person should refuse such bashfulness and avoid situations where bashfulness may be the cause by which you fall into sin.

They have to find for themselves a way to escape a critical situation tactfully or develop a strong personality so as to be able to defend their spiritual state in the face of resistance. They should at least be able to get away from company that puts them in critical situations and occasions in which they may be fought by the devil of bashfulness.

It is amazing that religious people are shy of their 'religiousness' being revealed while sinners boldly proclaim and perform their sinful acts, condemning those who have a higher level of spirituality.

24. Wasted time (Procrastination).

The devil desires to waste the period of time in which a man is alive.

Wasted time is the time which passes by without providing you with any benefit; no spiritual benefit, no mental or physical benefit and no benefit for others. The devil is not anxious to make you sin during this time; it is sufficient that you have wasted this time without gaining 'fruit' for yourself or others.

Many and varied are the examples of this kind of warfare.

Consider the long conversations we have without any objective, in which the people involve talk about redundant and pointless matters. Add to this uncalled-for visits and nights out, excessive luxury, as well as other means of amusement that use up our time and hinder the important (and beneficial) parts of our lives. We have heard of the people who pass their time at café's; playing all kinds of games and chatting just to 'kill time'. Whoever chooses to waste his time will look upon his life and consider it to be and have been of little value!

25. The devil employs supporters.

The devil never works alone; he has those who support his work, be it those from among his army of devils or men who knowingly or unknowingly support him – they may come in the form of friends, relatives, acquaintances, or even strangers. The devil was able to speak to the Lord, through the mouths of some of those who stood before the cross saying, *"If You are the Son of God, come down from the cross..."* (Matt. 27:40).

Do not disregard the warning that even your relatives may lead you astray, for it is said, *"...a man's enemies will be those of his own household."* (Matt. 10:36).

The devil may inspire one of your most beloved relatives to give you advice which will destroy your life, or he may cause them to resist your spiritual way of life, your desire to consecrate your-self to God and your time of worship and prayer. It is even possible for him to employ them to mock you. Therefore, be on your guard and examine well whatever advice you are given; holding fast to that which is good (1 Thess. 5:21). In saying this, do not say to any of your relatives, *"You are a supporter of the devil."*

Do not allow yourself to mingle with bad company, for they support the devil's aim (knowingly or unknowingly) to turn you away from God.

It is stated in the Bible, *"Evil company corrupts good habits..."* (1 Cor. 15:33). Thus, continually put before you the words of the first Psalm; *"Blessed is the man who walks not in the counsel of the ungodly, nor stand in the path of sinners, nor sits in the seat of the scornful..."* (Ps. 1:1). These 'seats' are the domain of the devil; avoid them!

Do not think that the devil appears to you only in a visible form to fight you.

This is an extreme degree of warfare of which God does not permit except for those holy people who are able to endure it. If the devil desires to provoke you, he will send you someone to do so; that person, for that instance, is of the devil's supporters. So too is anyone who tempts you; who leads you to sin, helps you on your way towards sin or causes you to fall into sin.

The wicked are the supporters of the devil.

The wicked congregate in the places of amusement and the places by which many are caused to stumble. The wicked include the countless atheist philosophers and those who call for atheism, who spread unsound and misleading doctrine with regard to God, spreading this ultimate kind of evil. Against this kind of evil David the Prophet and his men cried out, *"O Lord, I pray thee, turn the counsel of Ahithophel into foolishness."* (2 Sam. 15:31); this counsel of Ahithophel, during Absalom's uprising against his father David, was extremely harmful both to David and his men.

Consider how the devil overthrows the world into heresy. It is not necessary that he does so himself but he offers heresies to the world through his human supporters who spread them, explain them to people and call them to believe in such heresies.

So we have to pray at all times that the Lord may save us from the supporters of the devil; his angels, his troops, his assistants and supporters - and all those who do his will on earth - all the powers of the enemy.

Note:

a) With regard to fighting fearful visions, diabolic dreams and deceptions of the devil, we dealt with these in the second chapter of this book regarding the attributes and wars of the devil, under the two attributes 'cruel' and 'liar'.

b) The points we have mentioned are not an exhaustive list on the intrigues of the devil. His desire to commit evil does not wane nor do his intrigues end; he can invent a ceaseless number of new ways of committing evil. Undoubtedly, he has and will continue to adapt his wars and intrigues; may God have mercy on us and save us from him and them.

Let is remember the prayer in the Eleventh Hour Prayer; *"...save us from the temptations of the enemy and defeat all his traps set against us."* Amen.

CHAPTER 4

HOW TO OVERCOME DIABOLIC WARS

Our discussion regarding the devil's attributes and his various intrigues was not done in order that you might become fearful of him but rather that you might be cautious and guard yourself against him. For in spite of his violence and craftiness, overcoming him is both possible and easy.

1. Overcoming is possible.

If you continually believe and think that it is difficult or impossible to be victorious in your warfare against the devil, you will find yourself becoming faint and weakened; ready to yield to his desire of separating you from God. Do not have this mentality but on the contrary, when the devil fights you, be absolutely sure that you are able to conquer, otherwise God would not have allowed you to be fought in the first place.

Learnt to contemplate on the lives of those who conquered before you – the saints and martyrs.

Keep in mind the story of Joseph the righteous who conquered in spite of the difficult temptation he faced. In the lives of David and Samson, you can find for yourself the means by which sin attacked and overcame them; know the reasons of these falls and avoid them. The cautionary tale of their failings is intended for our benefit, so that we may learn to guard ourselves from the sins they fell into.

The Holy Bible and the history of the church provide for us various examples of 'conquering'.

We know, for example, that repentance is possible no matter the condition of the person. This is apparent from the stories of the repentance of the Saints, St Mary the Egyptian, St Pelagia, St

Baiessa, St Augustine and St Moses the Strong, as well as the repentance of Solomon the wise and Samson.

When we find ourselves in a detrimental condition and the devil fights us with despair, let us remember such stories and be both comforted and encouraged by them.

Consider the life of St. Anthony. From him we can learn how to conquer in spite of the violence, diversity and abundance of wars we face. In like manner, there is something to be learnt by contemplating the lives of the numerous saints of our church.

We must also remember that God has blessed our nature.

When God was incarnate and took upon Himself our nature, He blessed it. In the Gregorian liturgy, we address the Son with the words, *"You have blessed my nature in You."* This nature has thus become wholly able to overcome the devil. We have become the temple of God in which the Spirit of God dwells (1 Cor. 3:16). We have also become God's children; born from on high, through water and spirit (John 3:3, 5).

As we remember the power given to us, we should likewise remember the spiritual powers surrounding us.

We should remember that we are not alone in our battles, as God's Holy Spirit helps us and reproves us of our sins (John 16:8), teaches us all things (1 John 2:27) and guides us to all truth (John 16:13). How then can the devil overcome us if we have the communion of the Holy Spirit (2 Cor. 13:14) and the Grace of our Lord Jesus Christ (1 Cor. 16:23)? So, we live; not we ourselves, but Christ lives in us (Gal. 2:20). Add to this the fact that many angels surround us and are sent forth to minister to us; we who are the heirs of salvation (Heb. 1:14). Seeing that we are also encompassed by a great cloud of witnesses who have conquered, *"Let us lay aside every weight, and the sin which so easily ensnares us..."* (Heb. 12:1).

Let us also remember God's promises in order that we may be encouraged.

He says, *"...Lo, I am with you always, even to the end of the age."* (Matt. 28:20). *"If God is for us, who can be against us?"* (Rom. 8:31). He says to every one of us, *"I will not leave you nor forsake you... for the LORD your God is with you wherever you go..."* (Josh. 1:5, 9) and, *"...for I am with you, and no one will attack you to hurt you."* (Acts 18:10).

Let us remember God's promises to those who conquer in order that we may be motivated and zealous in our struggle.

Remember, for example, God's promises to the seven churches of Asia; *"To him who overcomes I will grant to sit with Me on My throne, as I also overcame and sat down with My Father on His throne."* (Rev. 3:21). *"He who overcomes shall be clothed in white garments, and I will not blot out his name from the Book of Life; but I will confess his name before My Father and before His angels."* (Rev. 3:5). *"To him who overcomes I will give some of the hidden manna to eat... I will give him the morning star... I will give you the crown of life."* (Rev. 2:17, 28, 10). Indeed, he that has an ear, let him hear these words which fill the heart both with zeal and power.

Let us also be convinced that it is God who fights for us.

However powerful the devil may be, what is he able to do before God's unlimited power? Though the devil be like a roaring lion, God is able to send His angel to shut the mouths of lions (Dan.

6:22). Truly, *"The battle is the Lord's,"* (1 Sam. 17:47). *"The LORD will fight for you, and you shall hold your peace."* (Ex. 14:14). Since it is the Lord who fights for you, do not be fearful of the devil and his forces.

2. Do not be afraid.

Do not fear the devil, for in spite of the multitude of his talents and intrigues, he is weak before God's children.

The Lord has made it clear that He, *"...saw Satan fall like lightning from heaven."* (Luke 10:18). The Lord trod upon him by the cross and thus he is no longer, *"...the prince of this world..."* (John 16:11) as the Lord said before His crucifixion, *"Now is the judgment of this world; now the ruler of this world will be cast out..."* (John 12:31). *"The ruler of this world is judged."* (John 16:11). Hence, the Lord says to us;

"Behold, I give you the authority to trample on serpents and scorpions, and over all the power of the enemy." (Luke 10:19).

The Lord's promise to us that we shall tread over the power of the enemy is a promise full of both power and comfort, a promise which removes fear from the heart. The church regards this divine promise of such importance that it places it at the end of the thanksgiving prayer in order that we may mention it in our prayers every day, every hour, so that we may not fear the devils or the power of the enemy.

The devil has no authority over us but rather the contrary - we have authority and power over him.

The devils are subject to us through the name of the Lord (Luke 10:17). The Lord made the casting out of devils the foremost sign performed by those who follow and believe in Him (Mark 16:17). Of course, the gift of casting out devils must first be preceded by victory in diabolic wars. Whoever is able to overcome the devil's temptations and enticements, standing steadfast against him, is feared by the devil and gains power over him.

There is a great sermon by St. Anthony recorded by St. Athanasius in his book **"The Life of Anthony"** regarding the weakness of the devils. Read this so that your hearts may be strengthened and you may learn not to fear the devil.

Learn from the examples of the simple monks who were not educated but were able to defeat and overcome the devil in the wilderness, such as St. Paul the simple. Meditate and contemplate upon the lives of the martyrs and confessors who completely overcame the devil's temptations, power and weapons. Know also that;

The devil only defeats the person who submits to him.

True are the words of the saying, *"It is the slaves who create the master(s)."* It is the 'humility' and willing submission of the slaves that allows the master(s) to prevail in controlling them. Such is the case with those who submit to the devil but those whom the Son makes free, they shall be free indeed (John 8:36).

The devil finds great joy when he finds someone who is afraid of him.

For in your fear you become weak before him and are easily turned to the right and to the left. You are convinced that you will certainly fall into his hands – thus, your spirit is broken and you yield to him without resistance. This is exactly what he wants from you; fear grants him power over you. However, be assured that the Lord Jesus Christ is there to overcome and advise us against fear;

"It is I; do not be afraid." (Matt. 14:27). *"Let not your heart be troubled, neither let it be afraid,.."* (John 14:27).

Do not be afraid, because God's power, acting within you, is vastly greater than the power of the devil fighting you outwardly. I assure you that the fear within you is of greater harm to you than the wars of the devil. Those who were afraid of Goliath the giant were weak before him and could not resist him. As for David, who was not afraid, he advanced towards him boldly, depending on the Lord's assistance. He thus was able to defeat him. The story of David and Goliath is a fitting analogy of the wars of the devils. Perhaps you wonder what the secret behind David's lack of fear was; if we turn to the psalms, he answers you himself with the words;

"The LORD is my light and my salvation; Whom shall I fear? The LORD is the strength of my life; Of whom shall I be afraid?" (Ps. 27:1). He goes on to say, *"Though an army may encamp against me, my heart shall not fear; Though war should rise against me, in this I will be confident."* (Ps. 27:3).

So, face the wars of the devil with a peaceful heart and fight the Lord's wars, knowing that you will be able to conquer with His assistance. How severe and frightening are the words in the book of Revelations regarding fear; *"But the cowardly, unbelieving, abominable, murderers, sexually immoral, sorcerers, idolaters, and all liars shall have their part in the lake which burns with fire and brimstone."* (Rev. 21:8).

The cowardly are put before the unbelieving, murderers and

idolaters!

You may ask, *"Why?"* Perhaps it is because the person who fears the devil and submits to him falls into all these sins; or because the person who fears the devil and submits to him will find themselves afraid on the last day because they have not resisted and conquered as the select have.

I wish that you would read the stories of the saints who did not fear the devils!

Read about St. Anthony, to whom the devils appeared in the form of lions, tigers and fierce beasts roaring in dreadful voices to frighten him that he might leave the wilderness; yet he was not afraid and would respond to their words calmly.

Read about St. Macarius the Great, who slept in a tomb, placing a skull under his head as if it was a pillow. When the devils spoke to the person to whom the skull belonged in a loud voice, asking him to rise with them, the saint was not distraught but raised his head a little from the surface of the skull and spoke to it saying, *"If you want to go, rise and go with them to hell."*

As for you, do not be afraid, for the devils will not fight you in the same way they fought the saint. Hearken to the comfort-filled words of St. Paul;

"God is faithful, who will not allow you to be tempted beyond what you are able." (1 Cor. 10:13).

God would not allow the devil to tempt you above what you can endure, *"...but with the temptation will also make the way of escape, that you may be able to bear it."* (1 Cor. 10:13). So, do not be afraid of the devils and their wars, whether they fight you with fear or sin. The devil may arouse a great tumult to frighten people but he cannot do anything to one who is a firm believer.

I compare the attacks of the devil with the story of the fox and the drum.

There was a drum hung to a tree which would make an awful sound when the wind causes it to moves. A fox passed by it and was alarmed by the noise; he was afraid at first, then he grew emboldened and attacked it. When he found it was empty from within, he laughed, despising the drum. We could also liken the devil to a big balloon which appears to be large but is overcome by a small pin.

The devil is 'all bark and no bite'. He tries - and sometimes succeeds in frightening you but he has no power and does not have the liberty to do whatever he wants.

Do not forget that there is God, the Almighty, who hinders and hampers the devil according to His will.

In the story of Job the just, the devil did not follow his own will but was confined to the scope which God allowed him (Job 1, 2). The devil is not so powerful that you ought to fear him. The mere sign of the cross causes him to flee from before your face.

The devil wants you to imagine that he is powerful but do not believe him.

Continually remember his repeated defeats before the saints. Remember those who have had the power to cast him out of those possessed by him and how he has always fled in fear before God's children.

3. Resist the devil.

It is good to remember the words of St. James the Apostle;

"Therefore submit to God. Resist the devil and he will flee from you." (Jam. 4:7).

The expression 'flee from you', presents to us the weakness of the devil, for the apostle did not choose the words, *"Resist him and he will **depart** from you."* but he said, *"...he will **flee** from you."*

The devil studies a person see what they are made of. If he finds them to be the kind that are easily made afraid, he amuses himself and makes a mockery of such a person, making him his 'toy'. If on the other hand he finds them to be both strong and persistent in their struggle, refusing to be conquered, the devil fears such a person and flees from them. Thus, resist the devil and do not be deceived by his power, for although St. Peter the Apostle says, *"Your adversary the devil, walks about like a roaring lion, seeking whom he may devour."* (1 Pet 5:8), he continues saying, *"Resist him, steadfast in the faith..."* (1 Pet. 5:9).

You ought not to be frightened by his 'roar' but you ought to resist him. Let your heart be as the heart of a lion; more powerful than he. When it comes to your mind that the devil roars as a lion, remember the words of Daniel, *"My God sent His angel and shut the lions' mouths..."* (Dan. 6:22). Stand against the devil strongly and firmly, resisting with all your power.

Do not be submissive but resist in the battle which is before you, as a good soldier of Jesus Christ.

Fight with all your power and seek God's help. I like the words of the canticle, *"Behold, it is Solomon's couch, with sixty valiant men around it, of the valiant of Israel. They all hold swords, being expert in war. Every man has his sword on his thigh because of fear in the night!"* (Song. 3:7-8). Learn how to fight all that comes to you from the devil. Let your sword be on your thigh and as the psalmist says, *"Gird Your sword upon Your thigh, O Mighty One, With Your glory and Your majesty, and in Your majesty ride prosperously."* (Ps. 45:3-4).

If the devil fights you with a thought or emotion, do not submit to it but resist.

Do not accept anything that he offers you. Do not open your heart or mind to him. Do not give your will over to him and do not be familiar with him but resist him with all your power. Resist his thoughts, his temptations, his lusts and all his trials. Be cautious that you do not slacken, lest you should hear the reproach of the apostle;

"You have not yet resisted to bloodshed, striving against sin." (Heb. 12:4).

Unto blood. Be like the soldier who, *"fights till the last bullet and last man."* Be sure that if you allow an opening the size of even a pinhead to the devil, he will take the opening as a chance to bombard you from all directions; he will go to great extents in order to cause you trouble. Thus, resist him and leave no opening for him to enter. However hard he argues in order to justify sin, do not accept his words.

There must be no discourse with the devil concerning sin: no argument and no debate.

Follow the advice of the saints - *"Do not deal with the person whom the devil sends to fight with you."*

When the devil offers you a sin, he desires for you to form a dialogue with the sin, to argue with it. He does this so that you may remain in its scope for as long a time as possible in order that you may eventually be influenced and overcome by it.

Thus, resist the devil at the outset - while the matter is still within your control.

If you delay in resisting him, his influence upon you will increase and your willpower shall decrease little by little. If you remain within the reach of the devil for an extended period of time, your resistance will fail, as was the case with Samson when he was pressed by Delilah daily - his soul was vexed unto death and he told her all his heart (Judg. 16:15-17).

Do not say, *"I shall bear with the thought to know its end!"*

You know very well its end, so do not deceive yourself. By opening your mind to the devil, you are being dishonest toward God. Thus, remove yourself completely from the devil, his ways and his principalities. Do not delay by indulging in his intrigues but push him away firmly, saying, *"Away with you, Satan!"* (Matt. 4:10), refusing him in all seriousness.

If you are able to firmly refuse all the thoughts of the devil, he will marvel at your ability to do so.

The devil, with his intelligence, knows very well the difference between serious resistance and the feeble resistance of one who is in two minds (1 Kings 18:21). He knows those who refuse him with a pure heart and those who refuse him in word alone.

The devil can easily determine who will resist him unto death and who will submit to him if he presses a little. Thus, resist in all seriousness, with all your strength and with all your heart.

I desire that you would not allow the devil to say that, *"You are softhearted."*

I do not want him to have the impression that you will rebel fiercely against him at the beginning but soon lose heart and respond favorably to his call to sin. Do not allow the devil to say, *"Though you object to my influence a great deal, in the end you consent to all the sins I put before you!"*

To resist is to refuse sin in all its forms and to accept nothing less than the perfection that God desires of you.

This also means insisting within one's heart to follow the spiritual path and to refuse any of the suggestions of the devil. Moreover, to be wary of the thoughts he places before you while they are yet afar off, without holding any form of dialogue with them. Dismiss such thoughts at first sight and shut the gates of the soul, the mind and the heart to them. Do not indulge in anything under the pretense that the matter is simple or that you will not be influenced by such a temptation!

Resistance is necessary but how do we do so? The Apostle Peter says, *"Resist steadfast in the faith..."* (1 Pet. 5:9).

4. With faith.

It is through faith that we conquer the devil but what type of faith?

It is the faith that God works with you, that God is able to annul the power of the devil and of all his snares set against you, the faith that God will not allow, *"...the scepter of wickedness..... rest on the land allotted to the righteous."* (Ps. 125:3). It is the faith that God is more powerful than all the intrigues of the devil and that God Himself fights for us.

"The battle is the Lord's," (1 Sam. 17:47); "The LORD will fight for you, and you shall hold your peace." (Ex. 14:14).

You must believe that the battle is the Lord's. It is not you who fights the devil but God fights him in you and with you. It is God who gives you the power to fight, the weapons which you use to do so and the wisdom to conquer the devils, as David the prophet says;

"Blessed be the LORD my Rock, who trains my hands for war, And my fingers for battle." (Ps. 144:1).

Do you take God with you in your wars, your temptations and problems? If you find yourself easily defeated, this may be because you do not take God with you. God is absolutely able to conquer in you and to be glorified in you no matter how slight your power may be and however weak your persistence, for the Holy Bible states;

"For nothing restrains the LORD from saving by many or by few." (1 Sam. 14:6).

When Hezekiah the king received the message of war from King Sennacherib, he placed the letter before the Lord, in the house of God, and poured out his spirit in prayer before God, asking Him to act. Thus, God intervened, sent His angel, and smote the camp of Sennacherib (2 Kings 19:35).

Consider how by faith David the prophet was victorious in his battles.

He says, *"If it had not been the LORD who was on our side when men rose up against us, then they would have swallowed us alive... our soul has escaped as a bird from the snare of the fowlers... our help is in the name of the LORD, Who made heaven and earth."* (Ps. 124). *"But my eyes are upon you, O God the Lord... Keep me from the snares they have laid for me, And from the traps of the workers of iniquity."* (Ps. 141:8-9). *"Refuge has failed me; No one cares for my soul. I cried out to You, O LORD: I said, "You are my refuge, My portion in the land of the living."* (Ps. 142:5).

With such faith, David conquered his wars as he conquered Goliath.

Just as David overcame Goliath, believe that no matter how powerful your enemy is, God will save you from them. Sing with David the prophet, *"The voice of the LORD divides the flames of fire. The voice of the LORD shakes the wilderness..."* (Ps. 29:7-8). Resist the devil with strong faith, repeating the words of St. Paul the Apostle, *"I can do all things through Christ who strengthens me."* (Phil. 4:13).

Be steadfast in this faith, trusting that God is on your side and will help you to conquer in all the wars of the devil - He will never forsake you. As He was with our fathers and led them to triumph in Him, He will be with you also and will not permit anyone to attack you or to hurt you (Acts 18:10).

This faith will give you strength of heart inwardly and a power over the devil outwardly.

Thus, when the Apostle speaks about our battles with the devils, he says, *"Finally, my brethren, be strong in the Lord and in the power of His might. Put on the whole armour of God, that you may be able to stand against the wiles of the devil."* (Eph. 6:10-11).

In our warfare, our personal power is insufficient. We must thus, *"...be strong in the Lord, and in the power of His might."* (Eph. 6:10). Our human weapons are not equal to the task; we must put on the whole armour of God and feel God's power working in us and for us.

With this power, we will neither have the spirit of failure nor the spirit of submission to the devil.

We will not have the spirit of slackening nor the spirit of despair - for God, upon whom we depend, is able to protect us against all diabolic wars. By this power St. Paul the Apostle was able to say, *"I have fought with beasts at Ephesus..."* (1 Cor. 15:32). With this power he was able to say, *"For God has not given us a spirit of fear, but of power and of love and of a sound mind."* (2 Tim. 1:7).

God's children never fail in their battles. They are valiant; neither the devil nor sin can prevail against them.

How encouraging is the statement which St. John the Apostle wrote about God's children, *"Whoever is born of God does not sin; but he who has been born of God keeps himself, and the wicked one does not touch him."* (1 John 5:18). All of them have the spirit of triumph and attain the promises as the Lord says in Revelations (Rev. 2, 3).

Look at Job the just and the Lord's testimony concerning him;

"There is none like him on the earth, a blameless and upright man, one who fears God and shuns evil. And still he holds fast to his integrity..." (Job 2:3). Could the devil prevail against such a person? No - God even used the example of Job to defy the pride of the devil.

In war, always put victory before you - not failure.

Say, *"It is impossible to fail as long as I rely God and He fights for me. I do not fear the devil but I shall say to the Lord, "Yea, though I walk through the valley of the shadow of death, I will fear no evil; For You are with me."* (Ps. 23:4). I am in the right hand of the Lord and He has inscribed me upon the palms of His hands (Is. 49:16). The Lord has said of His sheep, *"...And I give them eternal life, and they shall never perish; neither shall anyone snatch them out of My hand... and no one is able to snatch them out of My Father's hand."* (John 10:28-29).

5. With humility.

In the life of St. Anthony, he was able to defeat the devils on numerous occasions through his humility.

Whenever they gathered around him, he used to address them humbly, *"You strong ones, what do you want with me who am weak?"* and he would pray, *"Save me, O God, from those who think I am of any worth, though I am too weak to fight even the smallest among them."* When the devils would hear him raising prayers filled with such humility, they could not endure to be in his presence and would vanish like smoke.

St. Macarius the Great also, following the example of His teacher St. Anthony, conquered the devil with humility.

Once, the devil appeared to St. Macarius and said, *"We do all that you do! You fast and we eat nothing, you keep awake and we do not sleep. You inhabit the desert and wilderness and we also; but in one thing you defeat us."* The saint asked what that thing was and the devil answered, *"It is with your humility that you overcome us."*

Humility overcomes the devil for many reasons, among which are the following:

1. The devil is in no way humble – A humble person reminds him of his pride, which was the reason for his fall.

2. Humility reminds him of Jesus Christ, who emptied Himself and took upon Himself the form of a slave in order to save humanity. Merely the memory of this troubles him and causes him to flee.

3. The humble person, feeling his weakness, seeks the power of God to help him in fighting the devil - this is the thing which the devil fears most.

With regard to this theme, I once wrote in my notes the following words;

"The devil said to God, "Leave to me the strong, I can overcome them; but the weak I cannot overcome because when they find that they have no power, they fight me with Your power'."

The story of St. Sarabamoun the Veiled (Abu Tarhaa) proves that the ability to cast out devils can be empowered by humility.

The daughter of a certain ruler named Zahra was possessed by a demon and they brought her to the Patriarch in order for him to pray for her so that the devil might be cast out. The Patriarch said to them humbly, *"I do not have such a gift, go to St. Sarabamoun the Veiled."* When they went to him he said humbly, *"My prayers for her are not sufficient."* He required the cross of the Patriarch to cross her with and said, *"By the blessing of this cross, she will recover."* He meant by this to attribute her recovery to the Patriarch, not to himself. Thus, she recovered, for the devil could not bear such humility.

We have discussed the importance of humility in fighting the devils, considering the stories of a few saints. Let us now discuss an important question:

What is the practical effect of humility that helps in overcoming the diabolic wars?

1. A humble person realises their weakness and seeks God's help in all things; help which comes to them in abundance. Thus, they conquer because they do not depend on the weakness of mankind but upon God's providence.

2. The humble person guards themselves against the smallest sins and is afraid and cautious of any potential fall. Thus, they flee from all temptation, not throwing themselves into unwanted means of temptation and not considering any matter to be small. Through humility-driven cautiousness, they conquer the demons.

3. The humble person reveals his wars and points of weakness so that they are cured of their faults and thus conquer their wars.

4. The humble person continually prays and raises prayer even for the slightest of sins. Thus, they take God with them in their

warfare and conquer.

5. Humility itself is a virtue which the devils cannot bear and thus they make haste to flee before the face of it.

As a person conquers the devils by humility, he conquers also by wisdom and discernment.

6. Wisdom and discernment.

When a thought haunts your mind, you have to examine it well; is it of the devil? What is right about it and what is wrong with it? Do the same thing with visions and dreams, with the advice of others. Study it in the knowledge of all the methods applied by devils in order to deceive the children of God. St. John the Apostle draws our attention to such awareness, discrimination or discernment saying, *"...believe not every spirit, but try the spirits, whether they are of God."* (1 John 4: 1).

What then are the sources of such wisdom, knowledge and discernment?

There is a person who is wise by nature; God created them so, and granted them intelligence, wisdom and knowledge. They are able to uncover the wars of the devil and distinguish them from those thoughts which are spiritual and good. Another person acquires wisdom through the reading of the Holy Bible, spiritual books and stories of the saints. A third person acquires wisdom through experience; every fall teaches them a lesson and they become familiar with the wiles of the enemy so that they do not fall by them again. As one of the saints said;

"I cannot remember that the devils ever overthrew me in the

same sin twice."

A person may acquire wisdom through counsel, guidance and learning. As the person begins to distinguish the wars of the devil and reveal them, the person learns to flee from each individual sin and thus the enemy is unable to deceive them.

This all applies only to the person who desires to be victorious; for there is a person who knows that such a war is of the devil, yet he continues doing it for reasons within himself or because he is unable to resist.

As wisdom reveals the intrigues of the devil, it also provides the means of action.

A wise person knows how to escape the intrigues of the devil, how to escape his snares, how to rise after every fall and how to remove themselves from all means of sin.

If they do not know, wisdom leads them to consult others.

7. Counsel and confession.

Spiritual guidance reveals the intrigues of the devils and teaches us how to escape them.

The guide also acts as an intercessor, praying for the soul for which he is responsible, the soul which reveals their thoughts in order to be saved. As St. Paul the Apostle says, *"Obey those who rule over you, and be submissive, for they watch out for your souls, as those who must give account. Let them do so with joy..."* (Heb. 13:17). Heed this advice, for whoever follows his own will in the spiritual path more easily falls into the snares of the devils, as it is said;

"Those who have no guide, fall as the leaves of a tree."

Hence the importance of the father confessor in the church. You reveal to him your heart, to be ashamed, and to humiliate yourself before God in his presence. He guides you what you should do. Confession reveals wars of which beginners are perhaps not aware.

The person who confesses rids themselves of many sins.
The devils of the confessed sins cannot bear the humility of the person who confesses and thus flee. The devils also like to work in darkness, without anyone knowing what they are doing. By revealing their intrigues through confession they lose any power over you. Guidance breaks their snares and the dispensation given in the sacrament of confession ruins their labour. Hence, we find that the person who confesses his sins and obeys the advice of their guide learns to live a life of repentance and is saved from the diabolic wars. Though sin may not leave them entirely, its power against them is weakened.

Due to this, the devil seeks to hinder confession and attempts to foster a feeling of discontent within the confessor towards their confession father.

Here the devil of shame hinders confession. Then, upon finding this opening, comes the devil of lust, saying, *"What is the use of confession when you will fall into it again!"*. The devil of thoughts then begins to 'discuss' the subject of confession as a whole. Then follows the devil of doubt in order to foster doubt concerning confession and the confession father.

Be steadfast and confess all this too. Thus, the devil will be unable to find any way to approach you and will consider you a troublesome opponent and leave you.

8. Watchfulness and caution.

It is not enough to confess and reveal your inner state, asking for guidance but you ought to be watchful for your own salvation (see our book "Spiritual Watching and Vigil" for a detailed explanation) as the apostle St. Peter says;

"Be sober, be vigilant; because your adversary the devil walks about like a roaring lion..." (1 Pet. 5:8).

Be vigilant for your enemy is wakeful and strong, lest he should attack you during a time in which you are unaware, negligent or slackening, fatigued, at a time when you have forgotten your spiritual duty or when you are no longer anxious about your salvation.

The church provides us with many occasions on which it calls us to awaken:

During times of fasting it says to us, *"Be sober and ready."* and, in the Liturgies it says, *"Come and partake in the Holy Eucharist worthily."* In the sermons, readings and meetings, we are called to be anxious about our eternity and to fight God's wars with all carefulness. Thus, let us be watchful, heeding the words of the at the beginning of the Midnight Praises (Tasbeha), *"Cast away from our minds the slumber of sleep. Give us sobriety, O Lord, so that we may know how to stand before You at times of prayer."*

The devil wishes for his prey to be negligent so that they may be easy to destroy.

Whoever neglects their spiritual duties is easily made to fall, for they are not strengthened by any form of spiritual preparation or any spiritual inclinations which the works of Grace plant in the heart. Thus, sometimes when the devil seeks to overthrow a person, he begins with the weapon of neglect. The result is that the person slackens in their prayers, readings, spiritual meetings, confession and Holy Communion. As they become slack, the devil strikes them and they fall.

On the other hand, when the person is concerned with their spiritual duties, they put God before their eyes. This makes them ashamed of falling and God helps them in their wars.

There is a type of person that does not come to themselves except after falling.

An example of this type is the lost son who awoke only after being lost and remaining so for an extended period of time. David the Prophet also did not come to himself when he fell. He came to himself only when Nathan said to him, *"You are the man."* (2 Sam. 12:7). Solomon the wise was not in his wisdom when he fell and he was not aware that all was vanity and vexation of spirit until he had been enticed by women for the greater part of his life.

As for you, as long as your enemy the devil roars, declare war against him.

Say to the devil, *"Stop at the borders and do not breach them."* Prepare your weapons of fasting, prayer, vigil, repentance and caution. Hold on to the Lord and be watchful for every attempt of the enemy, every desire, every thought, every action of the senses. Do as St. Paul says;

"...bringing every thought into captivity to the obedience of Christ..." (2 Cor. 10:5).

In your spiritual vigil hearken to the words of the Apostle;

"Put on the whole armor of God, that you may be able to stand against the wiles of the devil..." (Eph. 6:11). Be wakeful, *"...[your] sword upon [your] thigh because of fear in the night."* (Song. 3:8). We mean by this the sword of the Spirit, the breastplate of righteousness and the shield of faith (Eph. 6) and all the spiritual weapons.

Let such caution and such readiness be with you all your life.

Be on guard unto death, and be watchful to the last moment, *"...lest, coming suddenly, he find you sleeping..."* (Mark 13:36). The Lord Jesus Christ was fought even on the cross when it was said to Him, *"If You are the Son of God, come down from the cross..."* (Matt. 27:40). So, be always ready then and do not say *"I have grown old,"* or *"I am already saved!"*.

Beware of the devil who fights against you with theology.

You may say, *"O Lord, have mercy upon me"* and find the devil rebuking you and saying, *"Never say, 'Have mercy upon me,' for the Lord had mercy upon you a long time ago when he redeemed you on the cross and saved you. What does this word 'mercy' mean then? It is a heresy!"* Say to him, *"The Lord had mercy upon me and saved my soul, but I have no mercy upon myself. I lose my salvation every day by sinning. So, I shall cry out saying, 'Have mercy upon me'."* Thus, watch for your own salvation.

In your watchfulness, behave in complete seriousness and caution.

Be very faithful even in the very little, for your faithfulness, caution and seriousness will cause the devil to flee from you, feeling that the battle with you is already lost.

There is an important weapon for victory against the devil and it is the most important weapon - that is, prayer.

9. Prayer and fasting.

When the disciples were unable to cast out the devil, the Lord said to them, *"This kind can come out by nothing but prayer and fasting."* (Mark 9:29).

Fasting and prayer are the means by which we achieve victory in our diabolic wars. They are the method by which we bring God into our lives and our wars, crying out to Him, *"...save us from the temptations of the enemy and defeat all his traps set against us."* (Absolution, Eleventh Hour Prayer of the Agpeya).

We will fail in our wars if we face the devil alone - without God.

We ought to say to God, *"This strong enemy of ours, who walks about as a roaring lion; he who is crafty and resourceful in performing works of evil cannot be overcome by our skill and intelligence - we seek salvation from You. We, as far as we can, try to discern the spirits, determine the thoughts that come from him and remain on guard against them but the power to do so is from You."*

We struggle as much as we are able to but You lead us to triumph in Christ.

In every sin, whether big or small, we do not want to face the devil alone; God must be with us. Thus, at the beginning of the First Hour Prayer we address Him with the words, *"... ask You to keep us this day without sin, and deliver us."* and in the conclusion prayer we say, *"Grant us to please Thee this present day. Protect us from every evil, every sin, and from every power of the enemy... Surround us with Your holy angels that we may be guided and guarded by them..."*

We must ask for God's help from the beginning.

Many people do not seek God except in times of affliction, acting in the same way as someone who does not go to the physician except when the disease becomes severe and they reach a critical condition. The church teaches us to pray for delivery before the wars come.

We should pray a protective prayer before a curative one.

We should ask God to annul all the snares of the devil set against us, not waiting until we actually fall into them and then ask God to get us out of them! Thus, in the Thanksgiving Prayer we ask God to take away from us, *"...all temptation, all the works of Satan... the rising up of enemies, hidden and manifest..."* We ask Him to take them away from us before they come; to *"...lead us not into temptation, but deliver us from evil."*

Let us not become confounded in the face of the enemy but let us ask for God's help.

Pray saying, *"This devil who is experienced in fighting people and has fought them for over seven thousand years I cannot overcome but You are God, the eternal, existing before the devil. He was the creation of Your hands before his fall. You know all his intrigues, you can tie him up and restrict him, set limits for him and even dismiss him completely. So save me from him."*

Thus, you must resort to prayer, without which you would not be saved.

If you fall in fighting the enemy know that your <u>prayers</u> have failed.

If your prayers are strong, you will certainly conquer him. Be sure that when God hears the cries of the poor, He will respond, for He says, *"For the oppression of the poor, for the sighing of the needy, Now I will arise," says the LORD; "I will set him in the safety for which he yearns."* (Ps. 12:5). So say to Him, *"Rise up, O LORD! Let Your enemies be scattered, and let those who hate You flee before You."* (Num. 10:35). Pray saying, *"Help, LORD, for the godly man ceases! For the faithful disappear from among the sons of men."* (Ps. 12:1). Rise and say openly, *"Gird Your sword upon Your thigh, O Mighty One, With Your glory and Your majesty; and in Your majesty ride prosperously,..."* (Ps. 45:3-4).

The devils were your enemies, O Lord, before they became my enemy.

They fight Your Kingdom in me and in others; so, fight them on my behalf and on behalf of others. Do not leave us alone in the wars of the devils for without You, we can do nothing (John 15:5).

David the prophet, who experienced God's triumph in his wars, wrote the words, *"The right hand of the LORD is exalted; The right hand of the LORD does valiantly."* (Ps. 118:15-16). Have you tried the Lord's Right Hand in your life? Have you experienced the salvation of God which was explained to Moses;

"Stand still, and see the salvation of the LORD... The LORD will fight for you, and you shall hold your peace." (Ex. 14:13-14).

If you experience this, you will find yourself saying with David the Prophet, *"The LORD is for me among those who help me; therefore I shall see my desire on those who hate me,"* (Ps. 118:7). *"A thousand may fall at your side, and ten thousand at your right hand; But it shall not come near you."* (Ps. 91:7). You have tried your own reasoning, your intelligence, your will, your own methods and the advice of others but have you experienced the Lord's salvation? Have you experienced the effectiveness of a strong prayer; prayer in which you take hold of the horns of the altar? If only you would do so!

Do not be like the person who says to the Lord;

"Let me work, O Lord, and if I fall and am not able to rise I shall seek you."

Why do you wait until you fall and are unable to rise? Seek him at this very moment and you will find his power supporting you so that you may not fall. Of course, if you do fall and seek God afterwards, He will lift you up but when you rise you will find yourself wounded and broken! Turn to the strong Hand, the only one that can truly protect you and cry out to the Lord saying, *"...save us from the temptations of the enemy and defeat all his traps set against us."* (Absolution, Eleventh Hour Prayer of the Agpeya). God will come to your help and deliver you and you shall find that you will sing with the psalmist;

"The snare is broken, and we have escaped. Our help is in the name of the Lord who made heaven and earth." (Ps. 124:7-8).

Ask then for God to give you the victory. He gave to those who struggled before you; Ask that He may give you power as He gave them and give you His Grace and the power of His Holy Spirit, that you may be embraced with His Divine power. Ask Him to rebuke the devil as He has done before and will continue to do and say to him, *"Away with you, Satan!"* (Matt. 4:10).

10. Away with you, Satan.

These words with which the Lord rebuked the devil, *"Away with you, Satan!"* (Matt. 4:10) were said not only to rebuke the devil during the time of the temptation on the mount but also to rebuke him for all his wars against mankind.

You shall truly experience the power of these words when the Lord comes in order to fight for you and removes the devil from your presence in order that his severe war against you may be stopped or - as with the temptation on the mount - so that he may depart from you for some time (Luke 4:13).

When you have a period of time that you are not experiencing any war or any troubling thoughts or any thoughts of lusts; when you are no longer fatigued but a new light shines upon you, know that the Lord has rebuked the devil and dismissed him, sending him away from you.

God does not permit the devil to fight us continuously.

God does not permit the devil to hold us in his grip. When God lets the devil tempt us, it is in order to give us the chance to gain spiritual benefit from these wars. However, when the devil presses on us with despair or confusion, God rebukes him saying, *"Away with you, Satan!"* (Matt. 4:10).

There are many cases in which a person is relieved of the

diabolic wars.

A person finds himself completely with God, happy to be in His presence, wondering how they had sinned before and how they could have fallen in the first place. In the midst of this spiritually comforting sphere, they realise that the Lord Jesus Christ, who Himself overcame these diabolic wars, had indeed rebuked the devil on their behalf. It is as if He has said to the devil, *"I gave you the liberty to tempt and try My child but not to this extent. 'Away with you, Satan!'"* (Matt. 4:10).

Believe me, brethren, the sins which we fall into form only a portion of the diabolic wars with which we could be plagued.

These vast wars would have pressed violently on us had not God stopped them from reaching us and had He not prevented the devil from tempting us with them. God only permits that you be fought with the wars which you can resist. If He permitted that you be fought with the others you would not be able bear it.

You may be exposed to a severe war and be about to fall but then you find yourself saved from such a war without knowing the reason why. This is because God intervened and said to the devil, *"Away with you, you have pressed on this person too violently."* This brings to mind how God put limits for the devil when he fought against Job; the first time, he was not to lay his hand on Job (Job 1:12) and another time he was not to touch his life (Job 2:6).

The words *"Away with you, Satan!"* (Matt. 4:10) are a great comfort to us.

They signify to us that the wars of the devil are limited and that he is not free to do whatever he wants with us. They awaken us to the fact that the devil himself is in the hands of the Almighty, who is able to rebuke him whenever He wills, to hinder him and set limits for him and even dismiss him entirely. Let us be sure that whatever wars we are exposed to are, by the providence of God, within our power, our ability and our patience to overcome; we can overcome them as long as this is what we want to do. God has given us power over the devil - we can say to him *"Away with you,"* and he will leave us.

However, there are many times we do not want to say to the devil, *"Away with you."*

Sometimes, we slacken in fighting him and give him an entrance to the abode of our soul. Other times we submit to him and become weak, delaying in removing him from our lives. Sometimes we enter into dialogue with him and lose our hostility towards him, having lost our conviction to shun him. We even find ourselves sometimes yielding to him or cooperating with him, refusing entirely to say to him, *"Get away."*

I even fear that some open their hearts and souls to him and welcome him!

Many cannot dismiss the devil and say to him, *"Get away,"* for a friendship has formed between them and the devil. There is, in a sense, a sort of deceptive 'love' or familiarity and there are ties which link them with him and subject them to his will. Even if the Lord rebukes him and he flees, they seek him and plead for him to return and help them! They do not want the devil to leave them!

Only a pure heart can rebuke the devil and say to him, *"Away with you"* and be happy when God rebukes him, while others have needs which only the devil can satisfy and thus they keep him and even defend him! The same happened with the Ephesians who defended the goddess Artemis (Diana) and her statue (Acts 19:28). For this reason we see that the Lord would speak to people before healing them, saying, *"Do you want to be made well?"* (John 5:6).

Hence, if God wills to dismiss the devil away from you, respond to Him.

Let your will be one with God's will in order to dismiss the devil from your life, no matter what this may cost you and no matter how much it troubles you when the devil leaves you, for the Holy Bible says, *"Faithful are the wounds of a friend, But the kisses of an enemy are deceitful."* (Prov. 27:6). The devil may kiss you, pretending that he loves you and fool you with the idea that he will make you happy by fulfilling your lusts and desires, in order that you may not dismiss him from your life - but know that he is preparing snares to destroy you! Do not believe him.

Go deep into your heart and your mind and say, *"Away with you, Satan!"* (Matt. 4:10)

When the Lord rebukes the devil, rebuke him also, truly and with all resolve and determination, abolishing any former relationship between you and him. Do not try to keep God and the devil in your life for, *"What communion has light with darkness?"* (2 Cor. 6:14). Do not make friends with the enemy of God and do not take part with him in any act. Remove all his possessions from your life, your house and your library; all his pictures, his books and magazines, all his means of amusement, his songs and stories, his agents and supporters. Say to him, *"Away with you, Satan, and all that belongs to you."* Shut before him all openings so that he may not return to you.

Dismiss the devil with all seriousness, continuously, and resolutely.

Let not your dismissal of him be weak, half-hearted and insincere. As the common saying goes, *"An eye upon paradise, the other upon hell!"* Be sure that listening to the devil, with all his intrigues, is a loss to you. Be cautious not to accept anything from him, no matter attractive it may seem for it could cost you your life and your eternity.

We will now discuss the means by which you can dismiss the devil.

11. Facing sin with the commandments.

Learn by heart a number of verses against the sins which fight you.

For example, when the devil fights you with anger, say to him, *"...for the wrath of man does not produce the righteousness of God."* (James 1:20); or repeat the words of one of the saints, *"Though the irritable person raises the dead, he is not accepted by God or by anyone."*

If the devil fights you with the lust of the eyes, put before him the words of the Lord, *"Whoever looks at a woman to lust for her has already committed adultery with her in his heart."* (Matt. 5:28).

If he fights you with adultery, remember the words of the apostle, *"Or do you not know that your body is the temple of the Holy Spirit..."* (1 Cor. 6:19). *"Do you not know that your bodies are members of Christ? Shall I then take the members of Christ and make them members of a harlot? Certainly not!"* (1 Cor.

6:15).

If the devil fights you with the faults of the tongue, put before you the verses of the Holy Bible, *"In the multitude of words, sin is not lacking."* (Prov. 10:19). *"Let every man be swift to hear, slow to speak, slow to wrath,..."* (James 1:19); and also say;

"Set a guard, O LORD, over my mouth; Keep watch over the door of my lips." (Ps. 141:3).

If the devil fights you with the love of the present world, face him with the words of the Holy Bible, *"Friendship with the world is enmity with God."* (James 4:4) and *"Do not love the world or the things in the world. If anyone loves the world, the love of the Father is not in him."* (1 John 2:15), *"And the world is passing away, and the lust of it."* (1 John 2:17).

Remember also what is stated in Ecclesiastes, in particular; *"Vanity of vanities... all is vanity and grasping for the wind... and there was no profit under the sun."* (Eccl. 1:2, 14, 2:11).

If the devil fights you with pride, remember the words of the Holy Bible, *"Pride goes before destruction, And a haughty spirit before a fall."* (Prov. 16:18) and *"God resists the proud, but gives grace to the humble."* (James 4:6), (1 Pet. 5:5).

This way of facing sin with the commandments is advice given by St. Evagrius.

We find this is something which is used extensively in St. Evagrius' poems in "The War of Thoughts" - which is available in the manuscripts of the monasteries. However, you can find for yourself some verses from the Holy Bible which you may use in your wars and learn them by heart.

"The word of God is living and powerful, and sharper than any two-edged sword…" (Heb. 4:12) **and it will have the desired effect.**

Be sure that when you remember the word of God it will surely have a restraining and healing effect within yourself. As the Lord has said, *"So shall my word be that goes forth from my mouth; it shall not return to me void, but it shall accomplish what I please, and it shall prosper in the thing for which I sent it."* (Is. 55:11). Try then the power of the word of God in the wars of the devil.

CHAPTER 5

BENEFITS OF DIABOLIC WARS

God does not prevent the devil from fighting us, but He takes our side in these diabolic wars and turns them to our spiritual benefit.

We read how St. Paul the Simple was happily living with St Anthony and was protected by his prayers yet after a while he asked St. Anthony to reside alone so that he might face the diabolic wars alone and gain benefit for himself.

What are the spiritual benefits which may be gained from diabolic wars? Those wars which the secluded hermits experienced in the desert and wilderness until they were able to devote themselves completely to the love of God and were then able to fight the enemy?

1. The first benefit is humility.

The more severely diabolic wars fight a person, the more they feel their weakness, eventually putting an end to their pride and instilling a feeling of penitence within them. They find themselves liable to fall and their will to be fallible. From this they acknowledge that sin *"...has cast down many wounded, and all who were slain by her were strong men."* (Prov. 7:26).

2. Prayer and holding fast to God, asking His help.

When a person is at ease, they may not seek divine assistance, because they may not feel an urgent need to do so. But, when the war against them is severe, they cry out to God to give them victory over their cruel enemy. Thus, feeling themselves to be weak, they hold fast to God in deep prayer, forming a strong relationship with Him. As He has said, *"Call upon me in the day of trouble; I will deliver you, and you shall glorify Me."* (Ps. 50:15).

3. Spiritual wars call for compassion towards sinners.

Whoever is not fought by the devils may be harsh towards sinners, condemning them when they fall but whoever has been fought and experienced the violence of the enemy is compassionate towards every sinner and prays for them. As St. Paul the Apostle says, *"Remember the prisoners as if chained with them; those who are mistreated; since you yourselves are in the body also."* (Heb. 13:3); he also says about the Lord, *"For in that He Himself has suffered, being tempted, He is able to aid those who are tempted..."* (Heb. 2:18).

4. Spiritual wars give the person experience.

The person becomes practiced in fighting and learns the warfare of a Christian, becoming acquainted with the intrigues and craftiness of the enemy. They attain experience through their rising and falling.

Consider how with students every success is preceded by an examination; examinations requiring experience of and exposure to the content, knowledge gained and refined by countless hours of preparation and struggling in order for the person to pass. Likewise, we find that whoever has fought the wars of the enemy and succeeded has gained experience. These spiritual experiences are a school from which graduates become spiritual guides who are able to help others, encourage them and reveal the wiles of the enemy to them.

5. These wars are a blessing through which we gain crowns.

True are the words said by one of the saints, *"None shall be crowned except the one who conquers, and none shall conquer except the one who fights."* Our endurance in withstanding the wars of the enemy, our struggle and our resistance - all this shows our love for the Lord and gains us crowns in heaven. As one of the fathers said, *"Crowns (medals) are not given in the war only to the soldiers who achieve victory, but also to those who were injured, as long as they did not yield to the enemy and struggled against him."*

6. These wars achieve within us the spirit of continual alertness and readiness.

As the Lord has said, *"Let your waist be girded and your lamps burning..."* (Luke 12:35). When a person feels that they are in the midst of a war, they will always be ready to fight, willing to perform all manner of spiritual practices - such as prayer, fasting, humility and taking spiritual counsel - in order to achieve victory. If on the other hand the wars were reduced, perhaps this would lead them to spiritual lethargy. Wars cause them to always be ready, always cautious and always on guard. The fear of falling causes them to become better prepared in order to achieve victory.

7. Spiritual wars cause us to become powerful and unafraid.

They who fear war are they who do not face it or do not fight but the person who experiences wars gains courage and boldness. The crowns which they gain encourage them to enter other wars and they do not fear failure. Does a student say, *"I shall not be examined for I am afraid lest I fail. I shall not even study or go to school!"* No, they face the examinations bravely, saying *"I shall overcome the difficulties involved in learning and examination."*

8. Spiritual wars are a school of faith.

In the wars of the spirit, we are granted to see the hand of God; to see how it helps us and achieves victory for us, how it is able to rebuke the enemy, as it did with David, who, despite his small stature, had the strength to be able to defeat Goliath the valiant. This instills within us deep confidence in God's love, in His care and work for us.

9. Spiritual wars also grant the devil 'equal' opportunity.

He has the opportunity to fight, with all his power, lest he should protest against God's children, saying, *"Why does the Lord reward them? If I had the chance I would overthrow them."* This is exactly what occurred in the days of Job; the devil was granted his opportunity but Job remained steadfast to his integrity (Job 2). God allows the devil to fight the believers but He also grants them power to conquer and disgrace the devil.

10. Lastly, spiritual wars open for us the doors of the Heavenly Kingdom and our success in them determines our rank in it.

Everyone is given their wages according to their labour and their struggle. So each believer should do their best to express their love for God through our struggle in the spiritual wars, for how else can our love be revealed except by testing it in the spiritual arena; and how would our ranks in the Heavenly Kingdom be determined without such trials? May God be with us in all our spiritual wars and lead us to triumph in Him.

Glory be to God forevermore. Amen

www.ingramcontent.com/pod-product-compliance
Lightning Source LLC
Chambersburg PA
CBHW032033040426
42449CB00007B/882